Childcare Act 2006: the essential guide

Ann-Marie McAuliffe
Alison Linsey
John Fowler

national
children's
bureau

Co-published in November 2006 by NFER and NCB

National Foundation for Educational Research
The Mere, Upton Park, Slough, Berkshire SL1 2DQ
www.nfer.ac.uk
Registered Charity No. 313392

National Children's Bureau
8 Wakley Street, London, EC1V 7QE
www.ncb.org.uk
Registered Charity No. 258825

© NFER and NCB 2006
ISBN 1 905314 25 6
ISBN 978 1 905314 25 6

The views contained in this document are the authors'
own and do not necessarily reflect those of the NFER
or NCB.

Layout by Patricia Lewis
Index by Indexing Specialists (UK) Ltd
www.indexing.co.uk

20 06000 451

Contents

About the authors   iv

Foreword   v

Preface   vii

Introduction   1

Part 1 General functions of local authority: England   11

Part 2 General functions of local authority: Wales   47

Part 3 Regulation of provision of childcare in England   53

Part 4 Miscellaneous and general   115

References   124

Further reading   130

Glossary   131

Index   132

About the authors

Ann-Marie McAuliffe is principal officer in the Early Childhood Unit (ECU) at NCB. She joined NCB in October 2001. During her time at NCB she has worked with both the Early Childhood Forum and the Local Authority Early Years Network. She has also worked directly on numerous policy areas including lobbying on the Childcare Act 2006. She manages the *Listening as a Way of Life* series, (which focuses on the views of young children). Ann-Marie has completed her Masters in Early Childhood Education at the University of Sheffield and has written for a number of journals and magazines, including *Nursery World*.

Alison Linsey led the development of NCB's parliamentary work, including lobbying on Bills passing through Parliament such as the Childcare Act 2006 and the Children Act 2004. Alison also worked on NCB's Child Impact Assessment project, with the Children's Legal Centre, producing child impact statements on Bills for parliamentarians. These analyse the potential impact of legislation on children from a human rights perspective. From October 2006 Alison has taken up the post of Parliamentary Adviser for Barnardo's.

John Fowler currently undertakes management work in local government and writes on education and children's services policy and legislation. He was deputy head of education, culture and tourism at the Local Government Association from 1997 to 2002. Experience includes: secondary school mathematics teacher, examinations manager, community education worker, parent, school, college and university governor, local authority officer, and local authority member. In recent years, he has written for the *Local Government Chronicle*, Croner's *Education Briefings*, *School Leadership*, *Education Law Journal*, *Governors' News*, *Governors' Briefings*, NFER's *ER Matters*, and the *Education Journal*. In this time he has been the main author, or contributed to, 12 books including books on the Education Acts of 2002 and 2005 and the Children Act 2004.

Foreword

The Childcare Act 2006 is a significant and wide-ranging piece of legislation that has implications for all those who are responsible for planning, running and using early childhood services. This accessible and independent guide provides a valuable pathway through the complexities of parliamentary drafting and will be of value both to those who provide services and to the parents and children who use them.

Over the past ten years there has been substantial investment in provision for our youngest children. Free nursery places are now available for all 3- and 4-year-olds, local Sure Start programmes have been set up in the 500 most disadvantaged communities, and these local programmes are now extending into a network of over 3000 Children's Centres. These developments are now central to the ambitious *Every Child Matters: change for children* agenda. Underpinned by the Children Act 2004, the overall focus of *Every Child Matters* is to improve outcomes for all children and young people, to reduce the gap between those who do well and those who do not, and to improve the coordination between agencies in how services are planned, commissioned, delivered and inspected so that they are more effective in responding to the needs of individual children.

The Childcare Act reinforces the Children Act in giving local authorities a duty to improve the well-being of children and reduce inequalities. It requires authorities to assess the need for childcare, and to secure sufficient childcare for those parents who need it – though not to provide it themselves if there are private and voluntary sector agencies who can do so. The Act includes a range of duties that should improve quality, including the introduction of the Early Years Foundation Stage, which covers the learning and development requirements of young children, improvements in the qualifications of the workforce, and changes to the system of regulation and inspection. But the guide quite rightly raises concerns about the viability of this mixed-economy model of provision, and questions whether such services are sustainable in the longer term.

The Act is a reflection of the Government's commitment to reduce and, if possible, to eliminate poverty, by encouraging as many parents as possible to find employment. Where the primary focus of the Children Act 2004 is children and young people, the Childcare Act starts from the needs of parents, seeking to ensure that, through the provision of childcare, they are able to work and are better able to balance work and family life. However, for the first time in legislation, authorities are required to have regard to the views of young children in developing provision – an important clause that was inserted after debate during the passage of the Bill through Parliament.

The Childcare Act 2006 is an important piece of legislation that could lay the foundations for universal services for young children. This guide provides a useful introduction to all aspects of the Act, looking at the new range of duties for service providers and local authorities in England and Wales.

Dame Gillian Pugh
Formerly chief executive of Coram Family and an advisor to the Department for Education and Skills

Preface

This guide introduces the Childcare Act 2006, the first piece of legislation solely devoted to improving services for young children, by providing an objective section-by-section analysis in plain English covering:

- what it says

- background information including the parliamentary debate

- implications for those working in the early years sector and childcare

- implementation.

The introduction of the Act's provisions will take place over several years. Information up to 9 November 2006 is included. Readers will need to check for up-to-date guidance and regulations issued by the DfES.

Who should read this guide?

The guide will be of use to the many professionals working in early years and childcare who need a succinct description of the significant changes that the Act makes to their working practices. Policy makers planning and developing new services for young children will also find the guide useful. The guide is not a substitute for the Act, and many readers in the course of their work will need to refer to the legislation although the guide will act as a signpost for the parts they need to understand.

This guide is aimed at:

- directors of children's services

- lead council members for children

- local authority officers working in children's services

- children's information services

- schools leaders (headteachers, deputy and assistant headteachers)

- extended service coordinators

- local, national and professional organisations working in the children's sector

- Ofsted inspectors

- lecturers and students in further and higher education

- Sure Start Children's Centres

- childminders

- nannies and other home-based childcarers

- day nurseries

- nursery schools and classes

- pre-schools and playgroups

- crèches

- parents.

Although not a legal text, the guide will be of interest to lawyers. The guide will provide background information to lawyers and alert them to the need to examine primary legislation. Academics will find the guide provides useful background information for policy research studies and course material for individuals undertaking initial training in children's services. We have not written a guide for working in early years and children's services, but the book will provide background information enabling students to understand the statutory framework that underpins their chosen field of work.

England and Wales

The Childcare Act 2006 applies almost exclusively to England. The only sections of the Act that apply to Wales are:

- Part 2, sections 22 to 30 (General functions of the local authority: Wales)

- section 101 (Provision of information about children: Wales)

- aspects of interpretation, commencement, and minor and consequential amendments and repeals.

Further information on Wales is given in Part 2 (see page 47).

Nomenclature

Throughout this guide the following abbreviations are used for ease of reference.

s.   section
ss.   sections
para.   paragraph

Subsection, schedule and chapter are always written out in full. Please note that s.1(5) means subsection (5) of section 1.

Feedback

The authors welcome feedback on this guide, and are also happy to answer queries about the text. The authors would welcome comments about the usefulness of the text and suggestions about future publications explaining legislation. Please email comments to John Fowler at john_fowler@btinternet.com

Thanks

Our first thanks go to you, the reader.

We are grateful for the scrutiny of legislation by MPs and peers during the Bill's passage through Parliament. Ministerial replies in Parliament have improved our understanding of the legislation and this is reflected in the text of the guide.

The guide relies heavily on *Explanatory Notes: Childcare Act 2006* (referred to as the *Explanatory Notes*) and the *Regulatory Impact Assessment* (RIA). For each document, there are three versions: on introduction of the Bill to the Commons, on introduction of the Bill to the Lords and following royal assent. We are indebted to the officials from the Department for Education and Skills (DfES) for their work in producing these documents and to members of the Bill team for clarifying, in discussion, a number of issues. Particular thanks goes to Edward Wagstaff at the DfES for checking the factual accuracy of the content.

We are enormously grateful for our colleagues who have reviewed the text and stimulated our thinking. In particular, we wish to thank Sue Owen, Director, Early Childhood Unit, NCB, Alan Parker, editorial consultant for NFER, and Christine Grice, Head of Access and Support Services, London Borough of Lewisham. We wish to place on record our thanks to the staff of the NCB and NFER. In particular, thanks are due to the NFER's Communications, Marketing and Information Services Department and the NCB's Publications Unit for their encouragement and perseverance.

Responsibility for the comments and judgements in this book remain with the authors. Although considerable experience of children's services legislation has been brought to bear on the guide, the book does not purport to give definitive legal guidance or interpretation of the law.

Ann-Marie McAuliffe
Alison Linsey
John Fowler

Introduction

The Childcare Act 2006 supports the Government's commitment, set out in *Choice for parents, the best start for children: a ten year strategy for childcare* (HM Treasury *et al.*, 2004), to:

- give every child the best start in life

- give parents greater choice about how to balance work and family life

- reform the regulation and inspection arrangements for early years provision and childcare for older children.

The two main objectives of the Act are to:

- improve the well-being of all young children and reduce inequalities

- drive up the quality of childcare provision while rationalising inspection and regulation to give parents assurance of a minimum national standard for the quality of this provision.

This legislation straddles the complex mix of provision in the early childhood sector, and impinges on all maintained, private, independent and voluntary providers.

The government paper *Choice for parents, the best start for children: a ten year strategy for childcare* (HM Treasury *et al.*, 2004) is pivotal to understanding the Act. HM Treasury published the strategy in late 2004 with three other departments: DfES, Department for Work and Pensions (DWP) and Department for Trade and Industry (DTI), thus signalling the importance of improving childcare not just for parents and children but also for the future economic prosperity of the country. The document is referred to as the *Ten Year Childcare Strategy* in this guide. The DfES and DWP published an action plan for the strategy in 2006 (DfES and DWP, 2006a).

What's in the Act?

The Childcare Act 2006 (together with the Work and Families Act 2006) takes forward legislative proposals from the Ten Year Childcare Strategy. The Act is divided into four Parts:

- Part 1 places new duties on local authorities in England

- Part 2 places new duties on local authorities in Wales

- Part 3 provides for regulation and inspection of childcare in England. This Part is divided into five chapters:

  - general functions of the Chief Inspector

  - regulation of early years provision

  - regulation for later years provision for children under 8

  - voluntary registration

  - common provisions

- Part 4 contains general provisions, for example on when the duties come into force.

Context

The Childcare Act provides the legislative framework for a number of interlinking initiatives being implemented in the early childhood sector. The legislation also reforms the registration and inspection arrangements for childcare for children over 5.

The Act sits within the framework of changes to children's services started by the Children Act 2004 and the Every Child Matters (ECM) programme. Policy developments such as the Ten Year Childcare Strategy and the Children's Workforce Strategy have put a spotlight on working with young children. The development of government policy and legislation in this area reflects both the lobbying from the sector to set in law the importance of children's rights and entitlements from birth, and the changes in society where more than half of mothers with children under 5 go out to work.

The Ten Year Childcare Strategy sets out the Government's ambitions in four key areas:

- **choice and flexibility**: giving parents greater choice about balancing work and family life, increasing the number of Sure Start Children's Centres and making changes to parental leave

- **availability**: an affordable, flexible, high-quality childcare that meets the circumstances of all families with children aged up to 14 (the Act now increases this entitlement to the age of 18 for disabled children) who need it

- **quality**: high-quality provision with a highly qualified workforce, all full daycare settings to be professionally led, the Children's Workforce Development Council to develop a new qualifications and career structure, a new framework integrating care and learning, new regulation and inspection regimes and better information for parents

- **affordability**: families to be able to afford flexible, high-quality childcare that is appropriate for their needs by increasing the free entitlement to early years provision and the level of the childcare element of working tax credit.

The Labour government's long-term goal to halve child poverty by 2010 and eradicate it by 2020 also forms the context to the development of this Act. A key driver to achieve this ambition is to get parents back into work. Hence childcare for working parents (or those taking up education or training) is provided for in s.6 of the Act. In addition, the mounting evidence showing the benefits of quality early childhood experiences on later outcomes for children (and a positive impact on society and the economy, through a greater proportion of people in work and less drain on health and other public services) has maintained a high level of interest at a political level, matched with sustained investment since 1998.

The drive to increase the quantity of childcare places to enable parents to get back to work has led to concerns about the quality of this provision, and the need for practitioners to improve quality continually as part of an ongoing process. This legislation does not address 'quality' on the face of the Act, due to the difficulties in defining the concept in law. However, it is expected to be writ large on the ensuing guidance. In the debate on clause 6 (now s.6 'Duty to secure sufficient childcare') the Minister (Lord Adonis) responded:

> *There is no intention whatever to dilute quality. Indeed, all the measures that we have in place on childcare seek to improve the quality of provision generally.*
> Hansard. HL, 2006j, c 39

Sustainability

Early childhood services have benefited from a huge rise in investment and profile since 1997. Initiatives such as Sure Start Local Programmes have been both commended for their impact on children and family life and also criticised for not reaching some of the most disadvantaged. Yet, with the new duties on local authorities under the Childcare Act, and very little, if any, additional resources to underpin them, there is growing concern about the viability of a mixed economy of provision and the sustainability of the private, independent and community sectors. Section 8 of the Act goes some way to reassure non-maintained providers of their position in the Government's plan to deliver flexible, affordable childcare, as it does not allow local authorities (LAs) to provide childcare themselves unless no-one else is willing to do so, or unless it would be more appropriate for the LA to provide it.

The challenge, as set out in the Ten Year Childcare Strategy, is to create an integrated, flexible, affordable, sustainable and high-quality childcare on limited resources with a highly qualified workforce. This is to be achieved through a staged process of implementation until the end of 2008 when all the provisions in the Childcare Act are due to have come into force.

Workforce development in the early years sector

The increased investment in the early childhood sector, with a view to expand childcare places and improve the quality of provision, has meant an urgent need for a larger, better-qualified workforce. In April 2005 the Government published the Children's Workforce Strategy, which contained specific challenges for the early years workforce:

• recruitment

• development and retention of the workforce

• strengthening interagency and multidisciplinary working and remodelling

• promoting stronger leadership, management and supervision.

It also set out the formal development of the new Children's Workforce Development Council (CWDC). This is now the sector skills council for those working across social care and early childhood, with close links to other sector skills councils such as Skills for Health, Skills Active (play) and the Training and Development Agency for Schools. CWDC has the lead role in taking forward the Government's Workforce Strategy.

Workforce development is a key area for improving the quality of early childhood services, as noted by the Minister for Children, Young People and Families (Beverley Hughes MP) during debates in Parliament:

the quality outcomes and quality experience for children are fundamentally dependent on the experiences that they have every day in their child care settings, which depends on the training, experience and quality of staff.
Hansard. HC, 2005e, c 306

This appears in the Act under s.13, which puts a legal duty on local authorities to secure information, advice and training to childcare providers.

Early Years Foundation Stage

The Childcare Act 2006 provides the first legislative framework for children from birth to five in England – the Early Years Foundation Stage (EYFS) – to support their development, care and learning. This provides an opportunity to standardise the approach for working with young children nationally, and offers enhanced opportunities to share effective practice and ensure each child has the same right and access to quality early years provision. The EYFS brings together the existing educational frameworks for young children – the Curriculum Guidance for the Foundation Stage (QCA and DfEE, 2000) and the Birth to Three Matters Framework (DfES, 2002) – with the National Standards for Under 8s Daycare and Childminding (DfES and DWP, 2003). The EYFS is due to be published in February 2007 and will be mandatory from September 2008.

Regulation and inspection

The Childcare Act sets out two registers in s.32:

- the Early Years Register (EYR) for all providers working with children aged from birth to 5, who must deliver the EYFS

- the later years register – the Ofsted Childcare Register (OCR) – which has two parts:

  - the voluntary OCR, which is for providers of childcare for the over eights and will be operational from April 2007

  - the compulsory OCR for childcare for children aged 5 to 7, which comes into force in September 2008.

During the consultation on the Childcare Bill, the Government proposed to exempt childcare provision for the over fives (except childminding) from regulation and inspection. This prompted an exceptionally negative response from the children's sector. It was felt that the proposed arrangements would not safeguard the welfare of children nor ensure the quality of provision. This was taken on board and has been reflected in the development of the new Ofsted Childcare Register (OCR), and in particular in the development of the compulsory OCR.

The new OCR is aimed at encouraging a wider range of providers, especially out-of-school childcare and other activities, to be registered with Ofsted to give parents confidence to allow their children to attend such services.

Passage through Parliament

The Childcare Bill was introduced to the House of Commons on 15 November 2005 by Ruth Kelly (the then Secretary of State for Education) and Beverley Hughes MP, the Minister for Children, Young People and Families. Minimal changes were made to the Bill in the House of Commons except to bring the legislation in line with the measures going through Parliament in the Safeguarding Vulnerable Groups Bill (enacted in November 2006), and to add provisions on the collection of information about young children. In March 2006, the Bill passed to the House of Lords where it was led by Government Minister, Lord Adonis. Further changes were made in response to lobbying to:

- increase the age limit in respect of the duty on LAs to secure sufficient childcare from 16 to 18 for disabled children of working parents or those who are under-taking training

- place a duty on LAs to have regard to the views of young children (aged birth to 5) when carrying out their duties in relation to early childhood services in s.3.

On 11 July 2006 the Childcare Bill was given Royal Assent. The debates on the Bill during its passage through Parliament centred on fleshing out the details of the LA duties in Part 1, and on the requirements of the Early Years Foundation Stage in Part 3, Chapter 2. There was very little debate on Part 2 (General functions of Welsh local authorities) and on the provisions in Part 3 on the new regulation, registration and inspection regime for early years and later years provision.

A Regulatory Impact Assessment (RIA) to consider the probable impact of the provisions in the Bill on businesses, charities, voluntary organisations and the public sector was published by the Government alongside the Bill. This was updated when the Bill passed to the House of Lords, and the final RIA for the Act itself was published in August 2006 (DfES, 2006h). A separate Race Equality Impact Assessment was not produced in relation to the Act.

Implementing the Act

The Childcare Act 2006 will come into force largely in 2008. The LA functions in Part 1 will largely commence in April 2008. Duties on providers delivering childcare for children under the age of 5, including the Early Years Foundation Stage and the accompanying Early Years Register will begin in September 2008. In addition, providers caring for children under the age of 8 but over the age of 5 will need to be registered on the compulsory part of the OCR by September 2008. The voluntary OCR will start in April 2007. Transitional arrangements for providers who have to register under the Children Act 1989 but will not under the Childcare Act 2006 had not been announced by November 2006.

What the Childcare Act 2006 means for...

Disabled children

A 'disabled child' is a person aged up to 18 who has a disability as defined under the Disability Discrimination Act 1995. Local authorities will have to secure sufficient childcare for working parents suitable for disabled children from the ages of birth to 18, whereas for non-disabled children the cut-off is 14 years old.

Children and families from black and other minority ethnic communities

The Act does not have an explicit requirement to meet the childcare needs of children and families from black and other minority ethnic communities. However, the intention behind ss.6 and 11 is that LAs must secure childcare that is suitable and inclusive of groups whose members may be disadvantaged.

Young children (from birth to 5)

Services for young children must be better integrated with a duty on LAs to improve the well-being of young children and reduce inequality. Care and education for children from birth to 5 will now be integrated into a single framework, and young children will also now be consulted on the design, delivery and development of early childhood services.

Older children (5 to 14)

Children over 5 and under 8 will have the assurance that those who are providing their childcare services must be registered on the OCR. For children aged 8 and over, providers will be encouraged to join the voluntary OCR register to ensure that the childcare provided meets minimum standards of quality.

Parents

Under s.12, parents are now entitled to an extended Children's Information Service, which provides information, advice and assistance about childcare within their area and other services, resources and support for children and young people up to the age of 20.

Workforce

The Childcare Act provides a new duty on LAs to provide information, advice and training to childcare providers. The Children's Workforce Strategy, being delivered by Children Workforce Development Council, will meet the further development requirements of the workforce as a whole.

Extended school services – primary and secondary schools

This legislation supports the government aim for all schools to deliver the core element of the 'extended school' offer, which includes childcare provision.

Local authorities

Local Authorities will need to incorporate the new functions under the Childcare Act into their Children and Young People's Plans (CYPPs). This legislation will also put an emphasis on monitoring and evaluating the delivery of services to young children and their families to ensure an increase in the quality of provision delivered.

Inspectors/Ofsted

The Childcare Act 2006 makes changes to the regulation and inspection framework. Therefore, Ofsted inspectors will need to adapt their inspection processes in line with the new requirements under this legislation. In addition, inspectors will need to be trained on the new Early Years Foundation Stage in order to inspect it from September 2008.

Early childhood providers

Day nurseries, nursery schools and classes, pre-schools, playgroups and Children's Centres will be required to deliver the Early Years Foundation Stage from September 2008. Providers must register on the Ofsted Early Years Register, except where the provision is for those over 3 in schools or is otherwise exempted. Providers in all settings will need to attend training on the Early Years Foundation Stage.

Childminders

Childminders working with children under the age of 5 will need to attend training on the Early Years Foundation Stage and will need to register on the Ofsted Early Years Register. Some childminders may want to care for older children as well and to do so will need to register on the OCR. This is compulsory for working with children under 8 and voluntary for childminders only working with children over the age of 8.

Nannies

It is likely that nannies who do not have to register as childminders will be exempt from registering on the Early Years Register. Nannies will be encouraged to register on the voluntary OCR.

Crèches

It is uncertain (November 2006) as to whether crèches (operating less than 2 hours a day) will be exempt through regulation from being regulated by the Early Years Register and therefore exempt from delivering the Early Years Foundation Stage.

Final note

Given the mounting research on the benefits of quality early years provision to children and to society, plus the committed investment from Government, it was inevitable that the entitlement to early childhood services would be cemented in primary legislation. This Act can be viewed as laying the foundations for universal provision, similar to those systems in other European nations, for all children from birth and a positive extension of the welfare state. As the Minister for Children, Young People and Families (Beverley Hughes MP) stated:

> *The Bill is important and exciting. It starts to redraw the welfare state in terms of what families can expect to be provided for them in their areas on a local basis. The focus is on quality, improving outcomes for children in early years and reducing inequalities. The Bill is an integral part of our 'Every Child Matters' programme, and it will ensure that every child has the opportunity to achieve their full potential.*

Hansard. HC, 2006a, c1033

Part 1

General functions of local authority: England

Part 1, Chapter 1: Duties of local government in England

Part 1 covers the duties on local government to:

- improve the well-being of young children

- reduce inequalities between children

- secure sufficient childcare for working parents who need it for children up to age 14 and up to age 18 for disabled children

- provide information to parents.

Local authorities are pivotal to achieving the Government's goals for the Act in Part 1, they are given three headline duties to:

- s.1: promote the well-being of young children

- s.6: secure sufficient childcare for working parents

- s.12: provide information, advice and assistance.

Local authorities also have a number of supporting functions that are supplementary or consequential to these duties. Table 1 (p.45) lists 29 functions. Nine of the duties are to 'have regard to guidance' issued by the Secretary of State. Many of the functions replace or build on existing functions.

This chapter summarises Part 1 of the Act, then considers it section by section.

Improvement of young children's well-being (ss.1 to 5)

Local authorities and their NHS and employment service partners (Jobcentre Plus) must work together to improve the well-being of all children up to the age of 5 and reduce inequalities between them. Local authorities must ensure early childhood services are provided in an 'integrated manner' in order to maximise access and benefits to families. This provides the legislative basis for the model for Sure Start Children's Centres.

Provision of childcare (ss.6 to 11)

Following an assessment of the local childcare 'market', LAs must secure sufficient childcare for working parents or parents preparing for work through education or training. The duty applies to children up to age 14 and disabled children up to age 18. In particular, LAs must have regard to the needs of families on lower incomes and those with disabled children. Local authorities must take the strategic lead in their local childcare market to plan, support and commission childcare from the local private, voluntary and independent sector providers. Local authorities can only provide childcare directly if no other person is willing to do so or it is appropriate for the LA to do so. Local authorities must secure the free minimum amount of early years provision for all 3- and 4-year-olds whose parents want it.

Information, advice and assistance (ss.12 and 13)

Local authorities have a duty to provide information, advice and assistance to parents up to their children's 20th birthday and to prospective parents. The service must be proactive in reaching those parents who might otherwise have difficulty accessing the information service. Local authorities must also provide information, advice and training to persons who provide and intend to provide childcare in their areas.

Miscellaneous (ss.14 to 17)

Existing legislation is amended to take account of the new arrangements for early years services, including the inspection of the new LA duties under the Act and the Secretary of State's powers to intervene to improve performance.

Interpretation (ss.18 to 21)

Important definitions are given for childcare, young child and early years provision.

New definitions

Part 1 contains many new statutory terms and definitions.

Definitions of terms that are already in common use, for example 'daycare', 'pre-school provision' and 'nursery education' do not appear in the Act, while 'childcare' is defined in s.18. Some new terms are introduced, such as 'early childhood services', 'early childhood provision' and 'early childhood provider'. Part 3 introduces the terms 'later years provision' and 'later years provider'.

Commencement

It is expected that Part 1 will come fully into force in April 2008 when the new duties on LAs will commence, the regulations will be in place and the statutory guidance published. Some provisions will come into force before this date and information published before November 2006 about commencement can be found on page 123.

Section 1: General duties of local authority in relation to well-being of children

Important new 'general duties' are placed on local authorities – to improve the well-being of young children (aged birth to five) and to reduce inequalities between them. See Box 1 for the text of s.1. Supporting 'specific duties' are found in s.3.

Box 1 Section 1: General duties of local authority in relation to well-being of young children

1. An English local authority must–

   (a) improve the well-being of young children in their area, and

   (b) reduce inequalities between young children in their area in relation to the matters mentioned in subsection (2).

2. In this Act 'well-being', in relation to children, means their well-being so far as relating to–

   (a) physical and mental health and emotional well-being;

   (b) protection from harm and neglect;

   (c) education, training and recreation;

(d) the contribution made by them to society;

(e) social and economic well-being.

3. The Secretary of State may, in accordance with regulations, set targets for–

   (a) the improvement of the well-being of young children in the area of an English local authority;

   (b) the reduction of inequalities between young children in the area of an English local authority in relation to the matters mentioned in subsection (2).

4. In exercising their functions, an English local authority must act in the manner that is best calculated to secure that any targets set under subsection (3) (so far as relating to the area of the local authority) are met.

5. In performing their duties under this section, an English local authority must have regard to any guidance given from time to time by the Secretary of State.

English local authorities

The duty applies to 'English local authorities' by section 1(1). Under s.106, these are defined as those authorities that have education and social services responsibilities: the London boroughs, metropolitan districts, shire counties and unitary authorities. The shire districts are not 'English local authorities' for the purposes of this Act even though they are 'English local authorities' for the purpose of categorising performance under s.100 of the Local Government Act 2003.

Every Child Matters

The new general duties sit within the ECM strategy and therefore the outcomes in s.1(2) by which 'well-being' is assessed in relation to children are the same as that in s.10(2) of the Children Act 2004. The outcomes in the ECM programme are to:

- be healthy
- stay safe
- enjoy and achieve

- make a positive contribution

- achieve economic well-being.

Guidance and commencement

Guidance will be issued under s.1(5). Consultation on the guidance is planned for December 2006 on the general LA role and that of NHS and Jobcentre Plus partners. The guidance will be formally issued in late 2007 for the new LA duty to commence in April 2008. There will also be guidance on the target-setting process and actions LAs can take to meet targets.

Target setting

Section 1(3) enables the DfES to set targets for each LA, which improve the well-being and reduce inequality between young children. Section 1(4) requires LAs to plan to meet these targets.

Further information about how the new section 1 duties will work can be found in the DfES document *Consultation on draft regulations setting out the process for setting statutory targets for local authorities under the Childcare Act 2006* (DfES, 2006a). The LA target-setting process will be a key driver for the changes in the Act. The target-setting process will be used to ensure the investment made in early years and childcare provision is mainstreamed and secured for the future (para.1.4) and will build on the existing role of the National Strategies and Government Offices in supporting early years services.

The objectives are to involve LAs fully in the target-setting process and to ensure that targets are not imposed centrally without appropriate discussion and negotiation at a local level (para.2.1). The draft regulations state that the Secretary of State cannot set targets more often than annually and that the targets must relate to the Foundation Stage Profile (FSP), which will become the Early Years Foundation Stage Profile in due course. However, the Secretary of State may impose different targets if those proposed by the LA are not sufficiently challenging. The targets will be at LA level. There is no power to require schools (or other settings) to generate targets at their level (para.2.7). The Government recognises that it is not appropriate to set child-level targets at such a young age.

Targets will apply to FSP results recorded 16 months after the targets are set. There-fore targets negotiated between September 2006 and March 2007 will apply to FSP results submitted in summer 2008. However, the first targets to be given statutory force under the first set of regulations under s.1 will be negotiated in autumn 2007 with the regulations published in summer 2007.

The target-setting work will be fully integrated into the existing process of support and challenge following the Standards and Priorities meetings between the DfES and each LA (paras.2.3 to 2.5). Strategies to meet the targets will be part of each LA's Children and Young People's Plan.

Two targets

Each LA, will have two targets (paras 2.9 to 2.23).

Improvement target, which will be based on increasing the proportion of young children who achieve a total of at least 78 points across the FSP with at least 6 points scored in each of the personal social and emotional development (PSED) and communication, language and literacy (CLL) scales.

Equalities target, which will be based on improving the mean score of the lowest 20 per cent of results so that the gap between that average score and median score reduces by the agreed target.

Strategies for improvement

The DfES will produce guidance for meeting targets. Local authorities' contribution to the current national Public Service Agreement (PSA) target (see below) is by focusing on the development of children in the most economically disadvantaged areas. The new statutory duty places emphasis on the five outcomes for children, and reducing inequalities between young children. So although LAs should still focus on economic factors, they will also have to address other barriers to poor out-comes and inequalities. The current DfES and DWP PSA target is to:

Improve children's communication, social and emotional development so that by 2008 53% of children reach a good level of development at the end of the Foun-dation Stage and reduce inequalities between the level of development achieved

by children in the 30% most disadvantages Super Output Areas and the rest of
England by four percentage points from 16% to 12%
(HM Treasury, 2004)

This target uses data from the Foundation Stage Profile from July 2005, and the first results will be available from December 2006. This existing target is likely to be adapted in light of the new statutory duty. The Minister stated during the passage of the Bill that 'we are reviewing how statutory targets should be set, and we do not intend to use the same form for those targets as is used for the current PSA' (Hansard. HL, 2006j, c. 18).

The new Early Years Foundation Stage Profile will be the basis for measuring this target year on year. Local authorities will be given guidance on how to recognise and address circumstances that are barriers to achievement for young children in their area, in order to reduce inequalities between those children and other children in their area.

The timeline for implementation of the new duties in s.1 is given in *Choice for parents, the best start for children: making it happen. An action plan for the ten year strategy: Sure Start Children's Centres, extended schools and childcare* (DfES and DWP, 2006a).

See s.3 on specific duties available to local authorities to fulfil the general duty and s.6 for LA management and planning of these new duties.

Section 2: Meaning of 'early childhood services' for the purposes of section 3

This section defines 'early childhood services', 'parent' and 'prospective parent'. 'Early childhood services' consists of the following five elements.

- Early years provision, which is defined (in s.20) as 'provision of childcare for a young child'. According to s.19 a 'young child' is aged from birth to 1 September after his or her fifth birthday. Childcare is defined in s.18 and includes education and any other supervised activity or 'integrated childcare and early learning'.

- Social services functions of the LA relating to young children and their families. The Explanatory Notes give the example of supervised contact and early intervention for families identified as needing support. Parenting classes for parents and prospective parents would also be included in this definition.

- Relevant health services. Examples given by the DfES are universal children's health services such as health visitors and midwifery, and also specialists such as speech and language services.

- Government-managed employment service, which is now part of the DWP's Jobcentre Plus, to help parents and prospective parents into work.

- Information and advice for parents: see s.12.

'Parent' includes those who have parental responsibility and those who have the care of a young child.

'Prospective parents', to use the Act's words, 'means a pregnant woman or any person who is likely to become, or is planning to become, a parent.

All services available to parents are to be available to prospective parents.

Section 3: Specific duties of local authority in relation to early childhood services

To complement the 'general duties' in s.1, s.3 places 'specific duties' on LAs. The specific duties state how LAs can use early childhood services to fulfil the general duty to improve the well-being of young children. This important section is reproduced in Box 2.

There are four specific duties. They are to:

- integrate early childhood services (s.3(2))

- identify parents who could take advantage of early childhood service (s.3(3))

- involve parents, providers and others in the planning and management of early childhood services (s.3(4))

- listen to young children (s.3(5)).

Box 2 Section 3: Specific duties of local authority in relation to early childhood services

1. For the purpose of their general duty under section 1(1), an English local authority have the further duties imposed by subsections (2) and (3).

2. The authority must make arrangements to secure that early childhood services in their area are provided in an integrated manner which is calculated to–

   (a) facilitate access to those services, and

   (b) maximise the benefit of those services to parents, prospective parents and young children

3. The authority must take steps–

   (a) to identify parents or prospective parents in the authority's area who would otherwise be unlikely to take advantage of early childhood services that may be of benefit to them and their young children, and

   (b) to encourage those parents or prospective parents to take advantage of those services

4. An English local authority must take all reasonable steps to encourage and facilitate the involvement in the making and implementation of arrangements under this section of–

   (a) parents and prospective parents in their area,

   (b) early years providers in their area, including those in the private and voluntary sectors, and

   (c) other persons engaged in activities which may improve the well-being of young children in their area

5. In discharging their duties under this section, an English local authority must have regard to such information about the views of young children as is available to the local authority and appears to them to be relevant to the discharge of those duties

6. In discharging their duties under this section, an English local authority must have regard to any guidance given from time to time by the Secretary of State

7. In this section–

   'early years provider' has the same meaning as in Part 3; 'parent' and 'prospective parent' have the same meaning as in section 2

Childcare Act 2006: the essential guide

In addition, s.3(6) requires LAs to have regard to guidance from the Secretary of State. It is expected that statutory guidance will be published in December 2007 prior to commencement of the new duties the following April. See Box 3 for more information about early childhood services.

Box 3 Early childhood services

The management of the collection of services called 'early childhood services' is the means by which LAs can achieve the objectives of the Act, namely the improvement of the well-being of young children in s.1. The LA is given specific functions in respect of early childhood services in s.3 and a management role with respect to other service providers in s.4. While the list of early childhood services is limited, s.5 does allow the definition of early childhood services to be altered to include other services, such as the LA education functions of special educational needs provision, meals and transport. The Act does enable these services to be available for the 'free entitlement' (see page 31) but there is nothing to stop LAs and other partners contributing services under the ECM partnership arrangements under s.10 of the Children Act 2004.

Duty to integrate early childhood services (s.3(2))

Local authorities must secure early childhood services in an 'integrated manner', i.e. the five early childhood services (care, family support, health services, employment advice and information) must be readily and easily available and offered as a complete package to children and their parents. This is the legislative basis of the Government's vision for Sure Start Children's Centres where childcare, health and employment services should all be available to young children and their parents, although LAs are not bound specifically to this model. See *Sure Start Children's Centre Practice Guidance* (DfES, 2005b) for further information.

This new duty is supported by s.4 of the Act, which places a duty on LAs and relevant partners to work together and pool funds, and by s.3(4), which requires LAs to involve and consult parents, prospective parents, early years providers and others in arrangements to deliver early childhood services.

Duty to identify parents to take advantage of early childhood services (s.3(3))

Local authorities must actively find and encourage parents to use early childhood services, especially those parents who are unlikely to use the services but who would benefit from using them. This new duty links with the general duty in s.1 to improve well-being, and to reduce inequalities. Through encouraging families not yet engaged with early childhood services to access services, inequalities may be reduced. The duty may be fulfilled alongside the new duty in s.12 to provide information, advice and assistance to parents and prospective parents through the expanded Children's Information Service.

Duty to involve parents, providers and others in the planning and management of early childhood services (s.3(4))

In making arrangements for providing early childhood services, and implementing those arrangements, the LA should take all reasonable steps to involve:

- parents and prospective parents (see Box 4)

- early years providers from both the private and voluntary sectors

- other persons, including companies, corporate charities and unincorporated associations (see page 58), in the local area whose work helps to improve the well-being of young children.

See s.8 for government policy and the role of 'other persons' in the provision of early childhood services.

Duty to listen to young children (s.3(5))

For the first time in statute, LAs must also have regard to the views of young children aged from birth to 5 in discharging their duties in relation to early childhood services (s.3(5)). This will give effect to Article 12 of the UN Convention on the Rights of the Child, which states that children have the right to give their views on matters that affect them, and that these views are given due weight in accordance with the age and maturity of the child. This new duty has led to a consequential change to s.176 (Consultation with pupils) of the Education Act 2002, which now incorporates the views of children aged under 5 (see s.103).

Box 4 Parents

The duties to identify and involve parents make clear that LAs must work with parents in planning early childhood services. DfES Draft Outline Guidance *Childcare Bill: Duty to improve well-being and reduce inequalities in outcomes for children up to 5* (DfES 2006b) (found at www.surestart.gov.uk/ _doc/P0002086.pdf, and referred to as DfES 'Draft outline guidance on well-being') states that the guidance under this section on parents will:

- enshrine the importance of parental input in governance of Children's Centres, and stress the need to facilitate the involvement of all parents, including those who may not have the confidence to take a formal role on a governing body, for example through parents' forums

- ensure that services for parents are considered in the development of each Children and Young People's Plan

- ensure that Children's Centres and extended schools practice guidance clearly articulates the expectations of support for mothers and fathers, and that progress towards delivery on high-quality parenting provision is explicitly monitored

- expect that the views of young children also be actively sought and taken into account.

The requirement to listen to children was added to the legislation following debate in the House of Lords. In moving the amendment, the Minister (Lord Adonis) stated:

the Government are committed to ensuring that the voices of even our youngest children are heard and are taken into account. It has always been our intention that statutory guidance should carry forward and build on the precedent already set by the current Children's Centre practice guidance, which sets out ways to explore what young children really think about their settings. ... The amendment requires local authorities to have regard to information about the views of young children where that is relevant in carrying out their duties under Clause 3. It will encompass all aspects of the design, delivery and development of early childhood services. However, by drafting the requirement in this way, we avoid the risk that local authorities will be compelled to try to engage young children on matters where meaningful consultation is simply not possible. ... We all know how easy it is for adults to make faulty assumptions about what is important to young children and

what they feel. … In seeking to ascertain the views of young children, local author-ities may undertake their own surveys or research, or they may use existing mechanisms—for example, the Listening as a way of life series of leaflets published by the NCB on behalf of Sure Start. Other voluntary organisations also have signif-icant experience in this area and will be able to help to take this forward.
Hansard. HL, 2006m, c.1011

An example of this in practice is in Newcastle, where young children from nurseries in the Sure Start Armstrong area took part in sensory walks using disposable cam-eras to give their views about the strengths and weaknesses of the local area. The children's views are being fed into the development of the Children's Centre in that area, and will act as a baseline to measure the impact of the Children's Centre over several years (Bryson, 2005).

Statutory guidance will be issued to local authorities. Section 3 is expected to come into force by April 2008.

Section 4: Duty of local authority and relevant partners to work together

Local authorities are under a duty to work with their relevant partners, which are defined in s.4(1) as the NHS Strategic Health Authorities and Primary Care Trusts and the employment service Jobcentre Plus, to deliver the general duties (s.1) and specific duties (s.3). Section 4(3) places a reciprocal duty on the relevant partners. This section provides the statutory basis for LAs, the NHS and Jobcentre Plus to secure the services on a single site – a Children's Centre, which is the Government's preferred delivery model. In the same way, s.10 (Co-operation to improve well-being) of the Children Act 2004 provides the statutory basis for Children's Trusts.

Under the Childcare Act there are only two relevant partners, while there are a much larger number in the Children Act 2004. Section 5 of the Childcare Act can be used to add new partners. Under the Children Act 2004, LAs are under a duty to 'promote cooperation' between partners. The Childcare Act uses the stronger duty to 'make arrangements' to work with partners.

Both Acts use the same words to describe how LAs can work with their local areas. Thus s.4(4) and (5) (s.10(6) and (7) of the Children Act 2004) enable LAs and part-ners to provide staff, goods, services, accommodation or other resources for early childhood services. The partners are able to establish a 'pooled fund' made up of contributions from partners to fund early childhood services.

Statutory guidance under s.4(6) will be issued jointly by the DfES, DH and DWP, and will include updated guidance on Children's Centres.

The DfES *Draft outline guidance on well-being* states that guidance on employment services will set out:

- the mutual advantages of LAs and Jobcentre Plus working together to deliver integrated early years services
- what integrated early years services could look like
- what is expected of local partnerships
- what Jobcentre Plus can contribute
- 'best practice' examples of cooperation.

And for health services:

- the mutual advantages of local authorities and NHS services working together to deliver integrated early years services
- maternity services that can be delivered through Children's Centres
- ways of promoting public health through Children's Centres
- 'best practice' examples of cooperation between LAs and NHS services.

Section 5: Power to amend sections 2 and 4

The Secretary of State can by order amend the definition of 'early childhood services' in s. 2 and make any consequential amendments in ss. 2 to 4. For example, if an additional service were added to early childhood services then s. 4 might be amended to include this new service in the list of relevant partners who must work together. See s.105 for the making of an order under s.5 using the affirmative resolution procedure.

Provision of childcare

Sections 6 to 11 describe the Government's plans for delivering childcare not just for young children (as set out in sections 1 to 5) but for all children whose parents work and want childcare for their children up to their 14th birthday and for disabled children up to their 18th birthday. Section 6 puts a duty on the LA to 'secure' (not necessarily 'provide') sufficient childcare. Section 8 restricts the LA's ability to provide childcare directly but s.6 encourages the LA to stimulate a childcare 'market' to meet the childcare needs of working parents or parents in work-related education or training. In deciding whether there is sufficient childcare, LAs must aim to meet the needs of families on lower incomes and those with disabled children. Section 11 requires the LA to assess the sufficiency of childcare at least every three years and (under s.9) allows them to commission childcare from local private, voluntary and independent sector providers. Under s.7, LAs must secure the free minimum amount of early years provision for all 3- and 4-year-olds whose parents want it.

Section 6: Duty to secure sufficient childcare for working parents

This section contains the second headline duty for LAs, namely to secure, as far as is reasonably practicable, sufficient childcare to meet the needs of working parents in their area. The full text is reproduced in Box 5.

In introducing section 6, the Minister for Children, Young People and Families (Beverley Hughes MP) stated that:

> *It is one of the main* [sections] *at the heart of the* [Act] *and it is crucial to what we seek to do in relation to childcare. It is about giving all parents a real choice about how they balance work and family life. Within that overall objective it is about enabling parents on the lowest incomes, and perhaps with the most difficult circumstances in terms of disabilities to lift themselves out of poverty and give their children the best start in life.*
> Hansard. HC, Standing Committee D, 4th sitting, 8 December 2005a, c.120

Box 5 Section 6: Duty to secure sufficient childcare for working parents

1. An English local authority must secure, so far as is reasonably practicable, that the provision of childcare (whether or not by them) is sufficient to meet the requirements of parents in their area who require childcare in order to enable them-

---

Childcare Act 2006: the essential guide

(a) to take up, or remain in, work, or

(b) to undertake education or training which could reasonably be expected to assist them to obtain work.

2. In determining for the purposes of subsection (1) whether the provision of childcare is sufficient to meet those requirements, a local authority–

(a) must have regard to the needs of parents in their area for–

(i) the provision of childcare in respect of which the child care element of working tax credit is payable, and

(ii) the provision of childcare which is suitable for disabled children, and

(b) may have regard to any childcare which they expect to be available outside their area.

3. In discharging their duty under subsection (1), a local authority must have regard to any guidance given from time to time by the Secretary of State.

4. The Secretary of State may by order amend subsection (2) (and subsection (6) so far as relating to that subsection) so as to modify the matters to which a local authority must or may have regard in determining whether the provision of childcare is sufficient.

5. Except in relation to a disabled child, this section does not apply in relation to childcare for a child on or after the 1st September next following the date on which he attains the age of 14.

6. In this section–

'child care element', in relation to working tax credit, is to be read in accordance with section 12 of the Tax Credits Act 2002 (c. 21);

'disabled child' means a child who has a disability for the purposes of the Disability Discrimination Act 1995 (c. 50);

'parent' includes any individual who–

(a) has parental responsibility for a child, or

(b) has care of a child.

Commencement and implementation

This significant new duty on local authorities is expected to come into force in April 2008. In preparation, local authorities must assess the sufficiency of childcare in their areas under s.11 (see below). Although the duty to assess will not come into force until April 2007, the DfES is encouraging local authorities to begin the assessment in Autumn 2006. Final guidance on s.6 is expected to be published in September 2007. See 'The childcare market' on page 34 and the integration of planning in the Children and Young People's Plan.

Statutory guidance on this duty will be pivotal in helping local authorities develop the childcare market. The DfES has produced a note *Childcare Bill: Duty to secure sufficient childcare* (DfES, 2006c).

Helping parents into work

Section 6(1) gives a reason why local authorities must secure sufficient childcare. It is to enable parents to take up or remain in work and includes education or training to help them obtain work. This reflects Government policy, supported by research, that:

> *Children growing up in households connected to the labour market are likely to have a better understanding of the link between educational attainment and its consequences for later life. Parental employment is also linked to improved performance in education when a child is older. For the adults involved, employment can bring benefits of increased self-esteem, extended social networks, a greater sense of control, and reduced mental health problems. These all can have positive consequences for children.*
> HM Treasury *et al.*, 2004

During debates on the Bill the Minister, Lord Adonis, clarified that as 'work' is not defined in the Act it takes its ordinary meaning, and so could include voluntary work where there is a continued commitment, rather than one-off activities. He also commented that 'work' is 'something over and above people's general life commitments or familial duties' (Lords Hansard, 26 April 2006, Col GC118).

Sufficiency and affordability

Except for the duty on LAs in s.7 to provide free early years provision for all children over a prescribed age and of a prescribed number of hours a week, the Act does not secure free childcare for children of other ages and circumstances. The intention is that working parents, for whom the LA will secure childcare, will pay for it, albeit the LA must use its influence over the childcare market to ensure that there is sufficient affordable childcare especially for parents who can only afford childcare through the childcare element of the Working Tax Credit (s.6(2)(a)(i)). This will require active engagement with providers. The DfES note *Duty to secure sufficient childcare* (DfES, 2006c) states that 'local authorities should consider the range of ways they can work with childcare providers to improve the affordability of childcare'.

Subsections (2) to (5) state how the LA will know when there is sufficient childcare provision. To use the words of the DfES (2006c) note *Duty to secure sufficient childcare* (para.5):

> *'Sufficiency' will be met when parents in the local area are able to find the child-care they need to enable them to work or undertake training to assist them to obtain work. This covers both immediate demand and a longer-term strategic approach to assessment of parents' likely requirements, both in relation to those parents in work, and those who wish to enter work and identify a lack of child-care as a barrier to accessing work.*

Subsection (5) requires that there should be sufficient childcare for children up to the 1st September following a child's 14th birthday. For the older children, this is likely to be met by extended school provision. For disabled children, the duty extends until the child's 18th birthday. The Government's original intention was that the duty to secure sufficient childcare should be available for disabled children up to the age of 16, but this was amended following lobbying on the lack of current provision for disabled children aged 16–18 during their transition from children's to adult's services. Section 6(2)(a)(ii) requires that childcare provision for disabled children is suitable.

The duty is complex; a lot more will be expected of local authorities than ensuring there are more places than children. Detailed statutory guidance will be provided on how to assess sufficiency. See s. 11 (below). However, the duty is not absolute. The local authority only has to secure a place 'so far as is reasonably practical'. The DfES (2006c) note *Childcare Bill: Duty to secure sufficient childcare* states (para.6):

> *Although a local authority must take action to meet unmet needs of local parents as a group, it will not be failing to fulfil the duty solely on the grounds that an individual parent's particular need is not being met at a particular time.*

Childcare needs of particular groups

Local authorities will have to consider the needs of particular groups for childcare. The Minister (Beverley Hughes MP) stated that LAs will need to consider the needs of childcare for black and other minority ethnic families:

> [T]*he Race Relations (Amendment) Act 2000 places a duty on local authorities to promote equality of opportunity. In practice, it means that they need to take account of the cultural background of children in service provision, and that of course covers childcare. We therefore expect local authorities to take into account the need to consider cultural factors when securing childcare, and the guidance will give information as well as examples that highlight the practical ways in which local authorities can ensure that childcare provision is inclusive and reflects the cultural backgrounds and needs of black and minority ethnic families within their local populations.*
> Hansard. HC. Standing Committee D, 4th sitting, 8 December 2005, c.128

The DfES (2006c) note on *Duty to secure sufficient childcare* asks (para.10) LAs to work with providers to secure childcare which is suitable and inclusive of groups whose members are often socially excluded. In addition to children from minority ethnic groups, the note mentions children of refugees and asylum seekers, and children from disadvantaged and socially excluded groups such as looked-after children, children with teenage parents, and families with a parent who is homeless, mentally ill, disabled, misusing substances, in prison or experiencing domestic violence.

Quality

During the passage of the Bill through Parliament concerns were raised about how LAs are to define 'sufficiency', particularly in relation to the quality of childcare places, affordability and sustainability. The Government believes that quality is addressed through the Act by Ofsted's regulation and inspections functions and the new Early Years Foundation Stage (see Part 3). More widely, the Government recognises the need to increase the qualifications and skills of the workforce through the children's workforce strategy, and by placing a duty on LAs to provide information, advice and training to childcare providers (s.13). In addition, LAs can encourage providers to engage in continuous quality improvement processes. Quality Assurance Schemes (see s.9) are mechanisms to support this, and can include an element of professional development. Local authorities can encourage providers to engage with continuous quality improvement processes as noted by the Minister for Children, Young People and Families (Beverley Hughes MP) in the debates in the Commons Committee Stage: 'I agree that there is value in the continuous improvement that a quality assurance scheme brings to professional training' (Hansard. HC, 2005e, c.307).

Sustainability

The sustainability of childcare provision, especially provision in the private and voluntary sector, was, and no doubt will continue to be, a much-debated issue. Government Minister Lord Adonis stated that not only are LAs restricted in providing childcare themselves except in limited circumstances (under s.8), but that:

> *Local authorities clearly have to understand the sustainability of childcare in their area ... the [s.6] duty has been placed on local authorities because they are best placed to understand local unmet need for childcare and to fine-tune support for providers, parents and the market. ... Local authorities, providers and Ofsted have told us that there is now evidence of over-provision; that is why we have shifted the focus of policy and funding away from setting targets for place creation at the centre, towards supporting local authorities to secure a good match between supply and demand.*
> Hansard. HL, 2006a, c.105

Section 7: Duty to secure early years provision free of charge

Section 7 requires LAs to secure free early years provision of a prescribed description for each young child over a prescribed age, that is the Secretary of State can state for how long (prescribed description) and from what age (prescribed age) early years provision is available.

This replaces and broadens the existing duty on LAs in s.118 of the School Standards and Frameworks Act 1998. Section 118 limits the Secretary of State to setting the minimum age (3 years from 1 April 2004 by the Education (Nursery Education and Early Years Development) (England) (Amendment) Regulations 2003 (England. Statutory Instruments, 2003c). In addition, the LA has to secure sufficient 'nursery education' under s.118, while s.7 requires them to secure sufficient early years provision for each child. The duty is not limited by the s.6 duty, which only extends as far as childcare for working parents, etc.

The requirement to secure provision for each child reflects the extent of current provision: DfES (2006k) *Provision for Children under Five Years of age in England: January 2006 (Final)* estimates 96 per cent of 3-year-olds and that all 4-year-olds take advantage of the free entitlement.

The free entitlement (from 1 April 2006) is 12.5 hours per week for 38 weeks a year, having risen from 33 weeks a year. The entitlement to a part-time early years place can be at maintained school nursery classes, LA-maintained or private nursery schools, day nurseries, playgroups and pre-schools, and with accredited childminders who are part of a quality assured network (see Part 3 of the Childcare Act when it is introduced in April 2008).

The plans for future provision are that by the end of 2007 LAs in pathfinder areas will be increasing provision to 15 hours per week, and will be producing best practice material on the delivery of this extended free entitlement. Some 2-year-olds in the pilot areas will also be able to receive free early years provision. By the end of 2008 the numbers of 3- and 4-year-olds able to access the 15-hour entitlement will have increased, and by the end of 2010 it will be available to all 3 and 4-year-olds at this level of entitlement (*Choice for parents, the best start for children: making it happen*, DfES and DWP, 2006a). Further information can be found in SureStart Guidance *A Code of Practice on the Provision of Free Nursery Education Places for Three- and Four-Year-Olds* (DfES, 2006f).

The LA must have regard to guidance issued under this section, and a revised version of the *Code of Practice* will be produced. The duty will be in force in all local authorities in April 2008.

Section 8: Powers of local authority in relation to the provision of childcare

Local authorities are given three powers to support childcare in order to comply with the duty in s.6 to secure sufficient childcare. The powers in s.8(1) enable the local authority to:

- assist any person who provides or proposes to provide childcare (this may include financial assistance)

- make arrangements with any other person for the provision of childcare (this may also include financial assistance)

- provide childcare directly.

The power to provide childcare directly is greatly restricted by s.8(3). An LA can only provide childcare if it is satisfied that nobody else is willing to provide childcare or, if someone is willing, that in the circumstances it is more appropriate for the authority to do so. Note that a maintained school's childcare provision is not to be regarded as provision made by the LA (s.8(4)).

Until the Childcare Act is implemented, LAs can continue to provide childcare generally as a consequence of making daycare for children in need, under s.18 (Day care provision for pre-school and other children) of the Children Act 1989. Section 8(5) of the Childcare Act allows LAs to continue to provide daycare for children in need only. The term daycare is not amended by the Childcare Act: s.18(1) applies to children below compulsory school age and s.18(5) to children of compulsory school age. A consequential amendment is found in Schedule 2 (see page 120), which restricts the extent of subsections (2) and (6) so that they apply only to Wales. In other words, LAs will no longer be able to provide childcare as a consequence of providing daycare for children in need. See s.10 for charging for provision made under s.18 of the Children Act 1989.

The LA must have regard to guidance issued under this section, and the duty will be in force in all LAs by April 2008.

Section 9: Arrangements between local authority and childcare providers

Section 9 gives LAs the power to impose requirements on childcare providers as part of any arrangements made where the LA provides financial assistance (under s.8). This could include an arrangement to ensure participation in an ongoing quality improvement process such as a quality assurance scheme. Leeds City Council's Early Years Service has a requirement that 'all current providers of nursery education funding ... sign up to the new conditions'. The following conditions have now been included in the Provider Declaration:

Agree to undertake a Quality Assurance Framework within 6 months of being included in the Leeds Directory of Early Education providers, and complete a Quality Assurance Framework within the period of three years from the date of inclusion in the Directory. Failure to do so may result in withdrawal of funding and removal from the Leeds Directory of Early Education Providers.

Local authorities must carry out their functions in a way that enables childcare providers to meet requirements placed on them. If childcare providers do not carry out their contractual obligations, LAs have the power to require the repayment of all or part of the financial assistance under s.9(3). This replaces the current LA power found in s.153 of the Education Act 2002

Section 10: Charges where local authorities provide childcare

An LA can charge for childcare where it provides childcare directly (under s.8). Section 10 is necessary to put beyond legal doubt the ability of an LA to charge for childcare. Similarly, s.29 (Recoupment of cost of providing services, etc.) of the Children Act 1989 enables an LA to charge for daycare provided under s.18 (of the same Act). Charging for daycare provided under s.18 of the Children Act 1989 (for children in need), must be done under s.29 of the same Act. Local authorities are banned from charging for 'free' childcare provided under s.7.

Section 10 does not address the issue of charging by a school governing body for directly provided childcare (see s.17). Guidance on this issue can be found in the Department for Education and Skills publication *Planning and funding extended schools: a guide for schools, local authorities and their partner organisations* (DfES, 2006j) .

The childcare 'market' and local authorities

The combined effect of ss. 6 and 8 to 10 is to create what Ministers and DfES documents refer to as the 'childcare market'. Section 11 provides the market information to drive the LA functions in the earlier sections.

The Department for Education and Skills has produced information for LAs in order to prepare them for this commissioning work (see www.everychildmatters.gov.uk/ earlyyears/implementation).

Section 11: Duty to assess childcare provision

Local authorities must assess the sufficiency of childcare provision in their area in order to carry out the duty to secure sufficient childcare under s.6. The first assessment must be made within one year of commencement. The duty is likely to come into effect in April 2007 and LAs will have to complete their assessments by April 2008 (the date when it is proposed that the duty to secure sufficient childcare comes into effect). Another assessment must be completed within three years (subsection (3)). In the meantime the assessment must kept under review (subsection (4)). The Secretary of State can make regulations, and provide statutory guidance, about the contents and publication of the assessment, and whom LAs must consult (subsections (5) and (6)). The assessment must cover children and young people up to the age of 14 and disabled children and young people up to the age of 18 (subsection (7)).

Section 11 replaces the existing duty on LAs in s.118A of the School Standards and Framework Act 1998 (as inserted by s.149 of the Education Act 2002). The main difference is that the 1998 duty required an annual assessment.

Section 11 must be read in conjunction with s.6. The Minister (Lord Adonis) stated that:

> *the assessment duty in* [section] *11 is crucial in enabling local authorities to plan and facilitate the childcare market. It is important that, if a child has a particular need, it is taken into account when local authorities work with their partners to secure childcare* [the s.6 duty].
> Hansard. HL, 2006b, c.116

Childcare assessments should be undertaken in the context of the Children and Young People's Plan (CYPP), which was introduced under the Children Act 2004. A CYPP is a single, strategic, overarching plan for children's trust arrangements at local authority level. Local authorities will therefore also need to refer to the Joint Planning and Commissioning Framework (see www.everychildmatters.gov.uk/ _files/312A353A9CB391262BAF14CC7C1592F8.pdf) and the Guidance on the

Children and Young People's Plan (see www.everychildmatters.gov.uk/_files/ 58A771D2F683214338B20DA1393F9B29.pdf).

It is envisaged that the assessments under s.11 will help to map supply and demand, and provide the information for local authorities to identify gaps and address them as part of the process of the review and publication of the CYPP.

The DfES produced draft guidance on assessments in August 2006 (see www.dfes.gov.uk/consultations/conResults.cfm?consultationId=1413).

In preparing the assessment and keeping it under review, LAs must consult the people set out in the regulations and guidance, and a draft summary of the assessment must be available for them to comment on. The people to be consulted include:

- children
- parents
- childcare providers
- persons representing children, parents and childcare providers
- persons with an interest in childcare and persons representing those with an interest in childcare
- persons representing local employers and employer organisations
- local employers
- neighbouring LAs
- schools
- further education colleges
- local Safeguarding Children Board
- the local authority's partners (as defined under s.10 Children Act 2004).

Regulations and guidance will also set out the matters that must be contained in the childcare assessment. The LA must divide its area into sub-LA areas, and for each of these areas must set out the following in respect of each type of childcare and each age range:

- the number of places required
- the number of places available
- the number of places required in respect of which the childcare element of working tax credit may be used

- the number of places available for which parents would be able to use the child-care element of working tax credit

- the times at which the childcare is required

- the time at which the childcare is available

- the range of session lengths offered by childcare providers

- the requirements for specialist care for disabled children and those with special educational needs

- the number of places available which are suitable for children who have special educational needs or who require specialist care due to a disability

- the number of vacant and unused places

- the range of charges for the childcare.

In respect of the above, childcare includes:

- childminding

- care that is available during the school term before and after the school day only

- care that is available throughout the day during the school term

- care that is available outside the school term.

The age-ranges of children are:

- 2 and under

- 3 and 4

- 5 to 7

- 8 to 10

- 11 to 14

- 15 to 17 (in relation to disabled children only).

The guidance published for consultation states that LAs must undertake a number of assessment steps:

- demand for childcare – knowing the demographics of the local population, understanding the local labour market, knowing about planned and proposed property development, parental demand, employers' needs, and price and demand

- supply of childcare including extended schools provision

- mapping supply to demand – taking into account location, affordability, specific needs of disabled children and those with special educational needs, the times at which childcare is available including flexibility for irregular patterns of working, the ages of children for whom care is available and the types of care available. This will also include identifying any gaps

- drafting and consulting on the assessment

- publishing, reviewing and repeating the assessment.

Section 12: Duty to provide information, advice and assistance (to parents and prospective parents)

This section takes forward proposals from the 2005 Schools White Paper (*Higher Standards, Better Schools for All*) (GB. Parliament. HoC, 2005) to extend the remit of the Children's Information Service (CIS). Every LA currently has a CIS that provides information on all local childcare, early education and other care and support services for children and parents. The main change is that CIS will have to provide information about any other services, facilities or any publications that may be of benefit to parents, children and young people in their area. This extends the CIS's remit to include information for young people up to the age of 20.

The duty under the Childcare Act specifies that local authorities must provide information, advice and assistance to parents and prospective parents who use, or propose to use childcare in that LA area. The service provided must include information about childcare, services, facilities or publications of benefit to parents and prospective parents, and services, facilities or publications of benefit to children and young people up to the age of 20. Local authorities must have specific regard to the needs of parents of disabled children and young people for information on childcare suitable for disabled children, and other services, facilities or publications which may be of particular benefit to disabled children and young people themselves, and their parents. Disability is defined under the Disability Discrimination Act 1995.

Draft guidance was made available during the passage of the Bill through Parliament and further information about the contents of the guidance was also given by the Minister.

- *Opportunities for parents to participate in their children's learning will be specifically included in guidance. Local authorities will be required to tell parents about parenting classes and programmes available locally and family learning opportunities*

- *Information services will direct parents to any resources available – for example DVDs, leaflets, websites or telephone helplines*

- *Information on services to support disabled children and young people will include specialist medical services, therapy services and support services*

- *CISs must liaise with each other to ensure parents can access information they need about provision in other areas without having to contact them separately or travel to them*

- *Information must be accessible to fathers (including non-resident fathers), mothers, others with parental responsibility, carers, disadvantaged and excluded groups, e.g. black and minority ethnic communities, and to parents for whom English is not the first language*

- *For each childcare provider the CIS should collect and make available: contact details, type of provision, cost of provision, age range covered, whether the provider is registered with Ofsted, and how to obtain Ofsted reports. If the childcare is based in a school the CIS should also have information on the management and registration arrangements*

- *The types of services CISs should hold information on include: education and family learning, health and well-being, parenting (including support for parents), positive activities for young people including sports, play and cultural activities, youth work provision and staying safe. Information should include a description of the service, opening hours, cost and any criteria for availability*

- *CIS's should also offer a 'brokerage service' for parents who cannot readily find available childcare to meet their needs. The brokerage service could include contacting providers to explain the specific needs of individual families and explore ways in which these could be met; encouraging providers to be flexible; and matching parents' expectations to available services. The brokerage service should provide information about difficulties in childcare supply as part of the assessment under s.11*

- *The guidance will include a section on delivery including outreach services, delivery outlets, management and organisation of the CIS, quality and links with other services.*
  Hansard. HL, 2006d, cc.286–9

A public consultation on the draft guidance to be issued under this section was published on 2 October 2006. In April 2007 the DfES will publish final statutory guidance on the provision of information for parents on local and national services, including childcare. The duty itself will come into force on 1 April 2008.

Section 13: Duty to provide information, advice and training to childcare providers

Section 13 expands on and replaces the existing duty on LAs to secure information, advice and training on daycare and childminding. Under s.13(1), LAs will be under a duty, subject to regulations made by the Secretary of State, to secure information, advice and training to:

- childcare providers who will be registered under the new regulation and inspection system in Part 3 of the Act

- those who provide childcare in maintained schools, non-maintained special schools and independent schools, whether registered or not

- those who work, or intend to work, in childcare in schools and other settings.

Section 13(1) is a duty to secure, i.e. the LA does not have to provide the information, advice and training. Section 13(2) and (3) give the LA power to provide other information, advice and training to those persons listed in s.13(1), and to provide information, advice and training to others who do not fall into the above categories, but who provide or intend to provide childcare.

Local authorities must have regard to any guidance issued by the Secretary of State (due to be published in December 2007), and can levy reasonable charges for providing the information, advice and training under this section. It is expected that this section will come into force in April 2008.

Section 14: Inspection

All LA functions under Part 1 of the Act are subject to inspection by Ofsted. Section 14 uses the legislation in s.38 (Inspection of local education authorities) of the Education Act 1997 and applies it to the childcare functions of LAs under the Childcare Act 2006. This section is prospectively repealed, as is s.38 of the 1997 Act (for England), by the Education and Inspection Act 2006 (E&I Act). Ofsted will acquire wide powers to inspect LA functions in Part 8, chapter 4 of the E&I Act2006.

Section 15: Powers of Secretary of State to secure proper performance

All LA functions under Part 1 of the Act are subject to the Secretary of State's intervention powers to secure proper performance under the Education Act 1996 (ss.496, 497, 497A, 497AA and 497B).

Section 16: Amendments to the Children Act 2004

Two amendments are made to Children Act 2004 to ensure that the new LA functions in Part 1 of the Childcare Act 2006 sit within the arrangements for children's services established under the 2004 Act.

The Director of Children's Services (the LA officer appointed under s.18 of the 2004 Act to carry out children's services functions) will have responsibility for the LA functions under Part 1 of the Childcare Act 2006. Consequently, the remit of the lead elected councillor for children's services under s.19 of the 2004 Act will include the Part 1 childcare functions.

The LA functions in Part 1 of the Childcare Act 2006 come within the Ofsted-led Joint Area Reviews (JARs) (defined in ss.20 to 22 of the Children Act 2004). This only applies to the LA functions, although periodic inspection by the Health Care Commission will cover the health service input to early childhood services. There is no provision for the contribution of Jobcentre Plus to come within the remit of JARs, which are a review of children's services. Jobcentre Plus is an adult service, although the work of the LA in making the partnership work will come within the remit of the JAR.

Section 17: Charges for early years provision at a maintained school

With very few exceptions, s. 451 of the Education Act 1996 prohibits charging for the provision of education during school hours for registered pupils at maintained schools.

Section 17 amends this provision to give a power to the Secretary of State to make regulations to allow charging for early years provision in certain circumstances. These circumstances will be set out in the regulations, but cannot include lifting the ban on charging for registered pupils of compulsory school age, or for provision under s.7 Childcare Act 2006 (the 3- and 4-year-old offer of 12.5 hours of free provision a week for 38 weeks a year from April 2006).

Charging for school education?

Regulations may be made that enable LAs and schools to charge parents for provision that is currently obtained free. Many children attend a maintained school full time for at least a year before they reach compulsory school age and virtually all children attend as rising fives. In January 2006, 98.1 per cent (126,650 pupils) of the rising fives in maintained schools were in full-time education (DfES Schools and Pupils in England: January 2006 (Final), Table 2a, SFR38/2006, 28 September 2006) (DfES, 2006l). The Act allows regulations to be made that enable parents to be charged for the time their children are in school in excess of the 'free entitlement' if the children are below statutory school age. The decision to charge will rest with the local authority, or if delegated, the school.

In defence of this new charging regime, the Minister (Maria Eagle MP) pointed out that schools can, under the existing arrangements, charge for childcare for children attending part time and that:

> *the clause is needed to prevent problems arising for schools as a result of the fact we are removing the distinction between education and childcare for early age groups.*
> Hansard. HC, Standing Committee D, 2005c, c217

Section 18: Meaning of childcare

Childcare is defined in s.18 of the Act as any form of care for a child (subject to exclusions below), and includes:

- education

- any other supervised activity.

Section 106 defines a 'child' as a person under the age 18.

A number of exceptions based on where the childcare is provided, and who is providing it, limits this very broad definition.

Childcare does not include:

- education, or any other supervised activity, provided by a school during school hours for a registered pupil over the age of 5

- any form of healthcare for a child

- care provided for a child as part of the establishment's activities (by a person employed by the establishment) within an appropriate children's home, care home, hospital in which the child is a patient or residential family centre

- care for a child detained within a young offender institution or secure training centre.

Childcare does not include care provided for a child by a:

- parent or step-parent of the child

- person with parental responsibility for the child

- relative of the child

- person who is a LA foster parent in relation to the child

- person who is a foster parent with whom the child has been placed by a voluntary organisation

- person who fosters the child privately.

The term 'childcare'

The term 'childcare' is made inclusive of education, at least for children under compulsory school age. This reflects the new Early Years Foundation Stage.

The definition emphasises the integrated nature of early years provision and corrects the misconception that education and childcare are two distinct activities for young children.

Section 19: Meaning of 'young child'

A child is a 'young child' for the period from birth until 31 August following the child's fifth birthday. Thus, a child might spend a year in a reception class while being a young child. This definition means that there is an overlap with the start of compulsory education under s.8 (Compulsory school age) of the Education Act 1996. Thus a child born on 1 September will be of compulsory school age on his or her fifth birthday but will continue in early years provision until the following 31 August. There do not appear to be any practical or administrative difficulties caused by the overlap of compulsory education and early years provision.

Section 20: Meaning of 'early years provision'

'Early years provision' means the provision of childcare (s.18) for a young child (s.19). This definition applies to Part 3 by s.96(2).

Section 21: Interpretation of Part 1

This section states that 'prescribed' means prescribed by regulations made by the Secretary of State.

Table 1 Local authority functions under Part 1

Duty	Section	Comment
To improve the well-being of young children and to reduce inequalities between those children	(1)	Builds on the duty in s.10 Children Act 2004 (CA2004) in relation to children aged birth to five. CA2004 does not impose a duty to reduce inequalities
To exercise functions to achieve targets set by the Secretary of State in relation to young children	1(4)	New duty; the s.10 CA2004 does not have a duty to achieve targets
To have regard to guidance from the Secretary of State about s.1 duties	1(5)	New duty but builds on the duty in s.10(8) of CA2004
To secure early childhood services in an integrated way, i.e. in Children's Centres, which is calculated to facilitate access and maximise the benefit of service	3(2)	New duty
To identify and encourage parents or prospective parents who would otherwise be unlikely to take advantage of early childhood services that may be of benefit to them and their young children.	3(3)	New duty
To encourage and facilitate the involvement of parents, prospective parents, early years providers, and other persons in the making and implementation of early childhood services	3(4)	New duty
To have regard to information about the views of young children in making arrangements for early childhood services	3(5)	New duty
To have regard to guidance from the Secretary of State about section 3 duties	3(6)	New duty
To work with relevant NHS and employment service partners	4(2)	New duty that builds on s.10 CA2004 but restricts 'relevant partners' to the NHS and employment service
To establish a 'pooled fund' with relevant partners (for provision of Children's Centres etc)	4(4)	New power that builds on s.10(6) of CA2004
To have regard to guidance from the Secretary of State about s.4 duties	4(6)	New duty but builds on the duty in s.10(8) of CA2004
To secure sufficient childcare for working parents	6(1)	New duty but builds on the existing duty in s.118A of the School Standards and Frameworks Act 1998 (SSFA)
To have regard to guidance from the Secretary of State about s.6 duties	6(3)	Replaces the duty in s.118A(6) of the SSFA1998

Table 1 Local authority duties under Part 1 *continued*

Duty	Section	Comment
To secure prescribed early years provision free of charge	7(1)	Replaces the duty in s.118(1) of the SSFA1998 to secure sufficient nursery education for children of a prescribed age
To have regard to guidance from the Secretary of State about s.7 duties	7(2)	Replaces existing duty in s.118(2) of the SSFA 1998
To assist persons to provide childcare, make arrangements with other persons to provide childcare or provide childcare directly	8(1)	Replaces powers in s.18 (2) and (6) of the Children Act 1989 (CA1989)
To have regard to guidance from the Secretary of State about s.8 duties	8(6)	New duty
To require childcare providers to meet arrangements for providing childcare	9(2)	Replaces power in s.153 of the Education Act 2002
To require payments for directly provided childcare in certain circumstances	10(1)	New power but complements the powers in s.29 of the CA1989
To assess childcare provision (1) of SSFA 1998	11(1)	Replaces existing duty under s.118A
To keep an assessment of childcare provision under review	11(4)	New duty required by the three-year planning cycle
To have regard to guidance from the Secretary of State about s.11 duties	11(6)(b)	Replaces existing duty under s.118A(2)(a) of the SSFA 1998
To provide information, advice and assistance to parents and prospective parents	12(1)	Replaces existing duty in s.118A (3) of the SSFA 1998
To have regard to guidance from the Secretary of State about s.12 duties	12(7)	Replaces existing duties under s.118A (4) of the SSFA 1998 and s.79V of the CA1989
To secure information, advice and training for childcare providers	13(1)	Replaces existing duty in s.79v of the CA1989
To charge for information, advice and training provided to childcare providers	13(4)	New power
To have regard to guidance from the Secretary of State about s.13 duties	13(5)	New duty
To comply with an order by the Secretary of State to secure the proper performance of an LA's functions under Part 1	15	New duty
To require the Director of Children's Services to support the LA in carrying out its duties under Part 1 of the Act	16	New duty

Part 2

General functions of local authority: Wales

Childcare in Wales

Part 2 (ss. 22 to 30) places general duties on LAs in Wales to secure sufficient childcare. These are very similar to those placed on LAs in England (see Table 2 for the equivalent sections), and cover:

- duty to secure sufficient childcare for working parents

- powers of the LA in relation to the provision of childcare

- arrangements between LA and childcare providers

- charges where LAs provide childcare

- power to require LAs to assess childcare provision

- duty to provide information, advice and assistance

- inspection and powers of the Welsh Assembly to secure proper performance, etc.

Table 2   The Part 2 sections and their England equivalents

Wales section	Section title	England section	Differences
22	Duty to secure sufficient childcare for working parents	6	Welsh LAs in addition must have regard to Welsh language childcare provision
23	Powers of local authorities in relation to the provision of childcare	8	Powers of LAs in Wales to provide childcare are not restricted
24	Arrangements between local authority and childcare providers	9	The same
25	Charges where local authority provide childcare	10	The same
26	Power to require local authorities to assess childcare provision	11	The Assembly may require LAs to assess childcare provision. In England, LAs must assess childcare provision
27	Duty to provide information, advice and assistance	12	The same
28	Inspection	14	The same
29	Powers of Assembly to secure proper performance, etc	15	The same
30	Interpretation of Part 2	21	The biggest difference is here: childcare is defined using the existing Children Act 1989 definitions of childminding and daycare, i.e. it does not include nursery education

Childcare Act 2006: the essential guide

Childcare Strategy for Wales

In November 2005, the Welsh Assembly Government launched the *Childcare Strategy for Wales: Childcare is for Children* (Welsh Assembly Government Department for Training and Education, 2005).

The main objectives of the strategy are to:

- ensure that childcare meets the developmental needs of children in Wales

- ensure that childcare is affordable and available

- provide childcare so that parents can balance work, life and family commitments.

The strategy set out to achieve these aims through:

- an investment of £12.5 million for childcare over three years

- a new statutory duty on LAs to secure sufficient childcare through the Childcare Act 2006

- introducing a programme of free childcare and family support through 'Flying Start' to extend free part-time childcare from 3- and 4-year olds to 2-year-olds.

Improvement of young children's well-being

Wales is not implementing the duty to promote the well-being of young children, early childhood services, and the Early Years Foundation Stage from birth to 5. Welsh policy is to create a Foundation Phase for education for children aged 3 to 7. The duty under s.25 of the Children Act 2004 (Cooperation to improve well-being: Wales) continues to apply (as of course does the equivalent duty in England under s.10).

Provision of childcare

Sections 22 to 26 set out the LA duty to provide childcare in Wales. The statutory definition of childcare is found in s.30 – it is a generic term using the existing definitions of daycare and childminding, and is therefore different from the England definition in s.18.

Section 22: Duty to secure sufficient childcare in working parents

Local authorities have a duty to secure sufficient childcare for working parents. It will operate in the same way as the duty on LAs in England under s.6. The duty applies 'so far as is reasonably practicable', and LAs will need to take into account factors such as the resources available to them.

When deciding whether childcare is sufficient, LAs must have regard to the needs of parents for childcare 'involving the use of the Welsh language' (s.22(2)(a)(iii)). This is in addition to having regard to the childcare needs of parents who are eligible for the childcare element of Working Tax Credit and parents with disabled children. Local authorities must also have regard to guidance issued by the National Assembly for Wales, and s.22(4) enables the Assembly to amend the criteria to which the LA must or may have regard in determining sufficiency.

The age range for which LAs have a duty to secure sufficient childcare is the same as that in England – up to the 18th birthday for disabled children, and up to the 14th birthday for all other children.

Section 23: Powers of local authority in relation to the provision of childcare

A Welsh LA can:

- assist any person who provides or proposes to provide childcare (including financial assistance)

- make arrangements with any other person for the provision of childcare

- provide childcare.

Unlike in England (under s.8) a Welsh LA is not restricted in its power to provide childcare. There is no intention to create a 'childcare market' in Wales.

Local authorities must have regard to guidance issued by the Assembly.

Section 24: Arrangements between local authority and childcare providers

Local authorities can ensure that any providers with whom they enter into a financial agreement meet any conditions imposed on them. Local authorities can also require repayment of financial assistance if providers fail to meet such conditions

Section 25: Charges where local authority provides childcare

Local authorities can charge for the childcare they provide except where provision is provided under s.18 (Day care for pre-school and other children) of the Children Act 1989, in which case s.29 of the 1989 Act applies.

Section 26: Power to require local authority to assess childcare provision

The Assembly can make regulations to require LAs to prepare assessments of the sufficiency of the provision of childcare in their local areas at prescribed intervals. The regulations may include the manner in which an assessment or review is to be prepared, and may require the LA to consult such persons as prescribed by regulations, and have regard to guidance issued by the Assembly.

Section 27: Duty to provide information, advice and assistance

Local authorities must establish and maintain an information, advice and assistance service for parents and prospective parents in accordance with regulations made by the Welsh Assembly. It is likely that information, advice and assistance should be available in the Welsh language. Welsh LAs must have regard to guidance issued by the Assembly.

Section 28: Inspection

Local authority functions under Part 2 of the Childcare Act 2006 may be inspected by Estyn, HM Chief Inspector of Education and Training in Wales.

Section 29: Powers of Assembly to secure proper performance, etc.

All LA functions in Part 2 are subject to the Assembly's intervention powers to secure proper performance under the Education Act 1996 (ss.496, 497, 497A, 497AA and 497B).

Section 30: Interpretation of Part 2

There is a different definition of 'childcare' in relation to Wales. Section 30 defines childcare as care that is required to be registered by the Welsh Assembly under Part 10A of the Children Act 1989, or care approved through a scheme made by the Assembly under s.12(5) Tax Credits Act 2002. In other words, childcare is child-minding and daycare using the definitions which apply pre-Childcare Act 2006 to England and Wales. These statutory definitions will apply only to Wales once the new definition of childcare under s.18 is implemented in England. There are two important consequences:

- 'childcare' in Wales does not include nursery education as it does in England

- the current registration and inspection system for daycare and childminding in Wales will continue and the arrangements in Part 3 of the Childcare Act 2006 do not apply.

Part 3

Regulation of provision of childcare in England

Introduction and background to Part 3 of the Act

Part 3 sets out to reform the regulation and inspection regimes for childcare and early years provision. This is the second of the Government's two objectives for the legislation.

History

The registration and inspection of daycare and childminding has its recent origins in the Childcare Act 1989, and the functions rested with local government. The Care Standards Act 2000 transferred these functions to Ofsted in 2001, and the legislation is found in ss.79N to 79R and s.79U of the Children Act 1989. The initial core of inspectors for childminding and daycare came from local government and were employees of Ofsted although they still had to be 'registered'.

Nursery education inspection outside maintained schools started with the Nursery Education and Grant-maintained Schools Act 1996. The law was consolidated in s.122 and schedule 26 of the School Standards and Framework Act 1998. Provision in LEA-maintained schools continued to be inspected as part of the normal school inspection, now under s.5 of the Education Act 2005.

In 1996, the Government's objective was to increase the supply of nursery education and stimulate parental demand with vouchers. In order to monitor this development and provide a means of recognising provision for the redemption of vouchers, Ofsted (the Office for Standards in Education) appointed nursery education inspectors. Inspectors had to be 'registered' and were mainly independent contractors.

The Education Act 2005 merged the nursery eduction and daycare and childminding inspectorates while leaving the inspection legislation in place. Ofsted, using either employees or inspectors contracted to Ofsted, carries out all inspections and publishes all their reports. In practice though, Ofsted has been managing a merged inspectorate since 2001 when s.79P of the Childcare Act enabled the combination of the two registers of inspectors.

The Childcare Act 2006 brings together in statute Ofsted's daycare and childminding and nursery education inspection and registration functions.

Why change?

The Government's ten-year strategy, *Choice for Parents, The Best Start for Children* (HM Treasury *et al.*, 2004) sets out a vision to give every child the best start in life. Parents are to have more choice about how to balance their work and family life. As part of the vision, the Government made a commitment to increase the availability, quality and affordability of childcare, which inevitably meant a review of the increasingly complex registration and inspection arrangements for this. Parents needed to be assured that their children were cared for in safe and suitable provision,

The Government has characterised this as follows.

> *Complexity and disproportionality in the regulatory and inspection regimes for childcare and early years services means that parents do not have the assurance that wherever their children are cared for they will be safe and well looked after.* DfES, 2005a

Change was supported by two cross-government reviews: the Gershon review, *Releasing Resources for the Frontline: Independent Review of Public Sector Efficiency* (Gershon, 2004) and the Hampton review, *Reducing administrative burdens: effective inspection and enforcement* Hampton, 2005) , which also required inspection regimes to improve efficiency, make the best use of resources and be proportionate to the risks involved.

Proposals were put forward in the DfES consultation paper *Consultation on Legislative Proposals for the Future of Childcare and Early Years Provision in England: Implementing the Ten Year Strategy* (DfES, 2005a).

The registers

The principle behind the regulation regime has not changed. Childcare providers are required to register with the regulator (Ofsted). Ofsted's role is to decide whether applicants are suitable for undertaking the proposed childcare. Subsequently, Ofsted has to inspect, and otherwise monitor, the childcare provision to ascertain that the provision meets a nationally agreed standard.

The proposal in the DfES consultation paper on the legislation (see above, DfES, 2005a) was to have two registers – an Early Years Register and the Ofsted Childcare Register (OCR) for school-aged children. The proposals for the Early Years Register have been translated into the Act and can be found in Chapter 2 of Part 3. Registration is compulsory for those providing childcare to children up to the 31 August after their fifth birthday.

Ofsted Childcare Register (OCR)

The DfES proposed that the OCR would essentially be a voluntary register funded by registration fees (unlike the Early Years Register). Voluntary registration would give the benefit of access to the Working Tax Credit subsidy and employer-based childcare subsidies. The latter register would require childminders for six- and seven-year-olds to register but the requirement to register 'group childcare' for children of this age would be removed.

Following consultation, the Government decided to divide the OCR in two: the compulsory OCR and the voluntary OCR. The compulsory OCR will now contain all persons providing childcare for 6- and 7-years-olds with the exception of provision made by schools. The original voluntary OCR is Part B.

The OCR, which in the Act is called the 'General Childcare Register', should be seen as a single register divided into two parts, rather than as two separate registers. An overview of the arrangements for the register are shown in Table 3.

Table 3 Arrangements for the register of childcare providers (adapted from the DfES consultation *Ofsted Childcare Register*, DfES and DWP, 2006c)

	Compulsory registration on the OCR (Part A)	Voluntary registration on the OCR (Part B)
Domestic premises	• Childminders looking after children aged 5–7	• Nannies • Childminders looking after children aged 8 and over only
Other premises	• Childcare providers looking after children aged 5–7 (but not childcare made by schools)	• Childcare providers looking after children aged 8 and over (but not childcare made by schools)
		• Exempted short-term occasional care or activity-based care for all ages (NB: the exemptions are subject to consultation, see page 66)

What's in Part 3?

There are five chapters in Part 3 as follows.

- Chapter 1 (ss. 31 and 32) gives responsibility to Ofsted to keep the Secretary of State informed about childcare provision and requires Ofsted to register and inspect providers.

- Chapter 2 (ss. 33 to 51) is about the Early Years Register (registration on which is compulsory for those caring for the under fives) and gives the statutory framework for the Early Years Foundation Stage.

- Chapter 3 (ss. 52 to 61) is on the compulsory Ofsted Childcare Register, which provides for compulsory registration for those caring for 6- and 7-year-olds.

- Chapter 4 (ss. 62 to 67) is on the voluntary Ofsted Childcare Register, which provides for voluntary registration for all other childcare providers.

- Chapter 5 (ss. 68 to 98) is about general provisions for all registers and additional powers of intervention, etc.

Table 4 shows where registration provision is found in the Part 3 of the Act and which kind of provision (childminding or other) may be found in sections of the Act.

Table 4   Where to find registration provision

	Chapter 2 – early years	Chapter 3 – later years, required registration	Chapter 4 – later years, voluntary registration
Register name	Early years register	Part A, General Childcare Register (compulsory Ofsted Childcare Register)	Part B, General Childcare Register (voluntary Ofsted childcare register)
Age range	Birth to 31 August after 5th birthday	1 September after 5th birthday to 8th birthday	8th birthday and over, exempted provision (except schools) and nannies

Table 4 Where to find registration provision

Provision	Chapter 2 – early years		Chapter 3 – later years, required registration		Chapter 4 – later years, voluntary registration	
	childminding	other	childminding	other	childminding	other
Requirement to register	s.33	s.34	s.52	s.53	n/a	n/a
Registration requirements	s.35	s.36	s.54	s.55	s.62	s.63
Entry on register	s.37	s.37	s.56	s.56	s.64	s.64
Conditions on registration	s.38	s.38	s.58	s.58	s.66	s.66
Requirements to be met	ss.39 to 48 – EYFS		s.59	s.59	s.67	s.67
Inspection	s.49	s.49	s.60	s.60	n/a	n/a
Report on inspections	s.50	s.50	s.61	s.61	n/a	n/a

In addition:

• Ofsted's duty to maintain the register can be found in s.31

• cancellation of, and disqualification from registration, and appeals can be found in ss.68 to 76

• Ofsted's powers to enter premises can be found in ss.77 to 79

• combining inspection reports can be found in s.80

• handling information by Ofsted, etc can be found in ss.81 to 84

• offences, etc relating to childcare can be found in ss.85 to 88

• miscellaneous information can be found in ss.89 to 98.

Definition of a 'person'

The Act refers to a 'person' providing childcare as, for example, in s.34(1) 'A person may not provide early years provision on premises in England unless …'.

This is the legal use of the term 'person', which means it can refer to an individual as well as a corporate body, such as a local authority, company, school governing body or a charity with corporate status. A person can also be an unincorporated association, which can include some charities, or just two or three people deciding to work together to organise daytime nursery provision or an after-school club. It can also be a person (in the ordinary sense of the word), such as a childminder, working by him or herself.

Part 3, Chapter 1: General functions of Chief Inspector

There are two general functions for the Chief Inspector in this Act: reporting to the Secretary of State on both early years and later years provision, and maintaining registers of childcare providers.

The Chief Inspector, Ofsted and HMCI

The responsibility for registering providers and inspecting provision is placed on the Chief Inspector, who is defined in s.96 as Her Majesty's Chief Inspector of Schools in England (HMCI). In common parlance the Chief Inspector is synonymous with Ofsted, which is the non-statutory name for the non-Ministerial Office of State embodied in the Chief Inspector.

For convenience, this Part refers to the Chief Inspector as Ofsted except when it is necessary to distinguish the Chief Inspector from Ofsted, in which case the term HMCI is used (see s. 77 on page 103).

Education and Inspection Act 2006 and Ofsted

The Education and Inspections (E&I) Act significantly enlarges the Chief Inspector's role. The legislation will establish (probably in April 2007) an Office for Standards in Education, Children's Services and Skills (which the Government will refer to as Ofsted). At the same time, the Chief Inspector's remit will be enlarged to cover children's social services and adult learning with a new title Her Majesty's Chief Inspector of Education, Children's Services, and Skills.

As the Childcare Act refers to the Chief Inspector, very few amendments will be required. The main amendment is to redefine who the Chief Inspector is in s.96. In addition, the E&I Act makes minor changes to ss.50, 61, 77 and 79 and replaces ss.14 (on local authority inspection), 31 (general functions), 80 (on combining reports) and 81 (on annual reports) with wider duties and powers for Ofsted.

Section 31: General functions of the Chief Inspector

Ofsted has a duty to keep the Secretary of State informed about 'regulated' early years provision including:

- the contribution of regulated early years provision to the well-being of children

- the quality and standards of provision

- how well the provision meets the needs of the range of children receiving provision

- the quality of leadership and management of the provision.

'Regulated' early years provision is defined as early years provision including the school-based provision that does not have to be registered under s.34. See s.96 for a definition of early years provision.

Section 31 also requires Ofsted to give advice to the Secretary of State on early or later years provision when asked to do so, but Ofsted may choose to give advice at any time. Note that, for this purpose, later years provision does not stop when children reach 8 years – the maximum age is subject to regulations by virtue of s.96(6)(b). See 'Upper age limit for 'later years provision' on page 93.

The four areas of reporting are the same as those found in s.50, where Ofsted has a duty to report following an inspection of early years provision, and s.61 where Ofsted has a power to report following an inspection of later years provision. The Ofsted report *Early Years: Safe and Sound* (Ofsted, 2006) is an example of the result of these inspection activities.

The legislation on Ofsted's reporting to the Secretary of State and on writing individual inspection reports (see ss. 50 and 61) is derived from Schedule 26 of the School Standards and Framework Act 1998 for nursery education inspection and s.79Q of the Children Act 1989 for childminding and daycare inspection. Nursery education inspections required inspectors to report in addition on 'the spiritual, moral, social and cultural development of children'. This is omitted under the Childcare Act 2006.

Reporting under the Education and Inspections Act 2006

New Ofsted reporting requirements can be found in s.118 of the Education and Inspections Act. They are expected to come into force in April 2007. Section 31 of the Childcare Act will be repealed. Ofsted will report on all activities under its new remit including:

- the quality of activities within the Chief Inspector's remit and (where appropriate) the standards achieved by those for whose benefit such activities are carried on

- improvements in the quality of such activities and in any such standards

- the extent to which such activities are being carried on as user-focused activities

- the efficient and effective use of resources in the carrying on of such activities and services.

There will no longer be a specific requirement on HMCI to report on the contribution of early years provision to the well-being of children and how far provision meets the needs of the range of children. In its place, Ofsted must report on whether provision is carried on as 'user-focused activities', a term which has yet to be widely used in childcare provision. In describing this term, the Minister (Phil Hope MP) stated its purpose is to 'send a clear signal to [Ofsted] that ... a user focus means that services should reflect the needs of those receiving them' and learned through speaking to children (Hansard. HC, Standing Committee E, 19th Sitting, Thursday, 2006b, cc911–912). The E&I Act does not amend the reporting arrangements in ss.50 and 61.

Section 32: Maintenance of the two childcare registers

Ofsted has to maintain two registers, although the second register is divided into two parts, corresponding to Chapters 2, 3 and 4 of this Part of the Act. They are:

- an Early Years Register (Chapter 2), which lists all those who are required to be, and are, registered as early years providers

- a general childcare register as described in the Act, but this book uses the Government's preferred term: the Ofsted Childcare Register (OCR), which is to be split into two Parts:
  - Part A of the OCR known as the compulsory register (Chapter 3), which lists all those who are required to be, and are, registered on the general register, who care for children over 5 but under 8 years
  - Part B of the OCR known as the voluntary register (Chapter 4), which lists childcare providers who are not required to register on the Early Years Register or Part A of the OCR and are not otherwise prevented from registering, i.e. Part B lists providers who have registered voluntarily.

Part 3, Chapter 2: Regulation of early years provision

This Chapter (ss. 33 to 51) sets out the registration and inspection requirements on early years providers (defined in s.96(3)), i.e. 'persons' (childminders and 'other' early years providers) who provide early years provision (defined in s.96(2) and s.20) for young children. A young child is defined by s.19 as a child from birth until the 31 August after his/her 5th birthday. Childcare is defined in s.18 (see page 43) as education and any other supervised activity.

This chapter regulates the childcare provision that is the lynchpin of the Government's objective of improving the well-being of under fives through integrated childcare and early learning using the Children's Centre model and the new duties on LAs.

Sections 33 and 34 state who should be registered with Ofsted on the Early Years Register, and ss.35 to 38 set out how a person registers with Ofsted and whether any conditions are placed on a person's registration. Sections 39 to 48 introduce the Early Years Foundation Stage (EYFS). A pivotal requirement on registration is that the EYFS must be provided. Sections 49 and 50 deal with Ofsted inspection of provision and the publication of reports.

Section 33: Requirement to register – early years childminders

A person cannot provide early years childminding unless he or she is registered on the Early Years Register. See page 58 for a definition of a person.

Early years childminding is defined in s.96(4) as early years provision on domestic premises for reward. If at any time the number of adults caring for children exceeds three then the provision has to be registered as 'other' early years provision under s.34.

Section 34: Requirement to register – other early years providers

For all other early years provision, that is provision which is not childminding, the registration is in respect of particular premises, and the person in charge has to register the provision. The person in charge can be an individual, two or more individuals acting as an unincorporated association, or a corporate body, be it a charity or a company. Large childcare providers might appoint a person in charge to run the provision. However, it is the employer who is required to register, not the employee who has day-to-day charge of the provisions, see s.97. See s.94 for a power that the Secretary of State has to amend legislation so that a person (most likely a corporate body) only has to make one registration when provision is made at multiple premises.

Exemptions to registration

The Act provides a number of exemptions to the need to register for early years and later years childminding. First are the exemptions found in s.18 where childcare is defined: these include childcare by a close relation or a foster parent, and childcare provided as part of any form of healthcare. Sections 33 (early years childminders) 34 ('other' early years provision), 51 (later years childminding) and 52 ('other' later years provision) give the Secretary of State power to make an order (see s.104) that lists other exemptions. See also page 66 for the exemption for schools in s.34.

The DfES has published a note on the likely exemptions (DfES, 2006g). This is subject to consultations in 2007 before the order is made (possibly in January 2008) and providers are required to be registered in September 2008. The exemptions follow closely the existing exemptions in s.79A of the Children Act 1989.

The principal exemption is likely to be childcare provision that takes place predominantly in the child's own home, e.g. nannies and babysitters. The DfES note remarks that to include this type of provision would be to intrude into 'family life and is unenforceable' but remarks that nannies and babysitters can join the voluntary part of the Ofsted Childcare Register (OCR) as can the other adults who provide exemptions. The DfES note states, 'we will ask Ofsted to encourage those providers for whom registration ceases to be compulsory to join the new register and continue to be tax creditable' (DfES and DWP, 2006c). See s.83 (page 105).

Other likely exemptions include:

- evening provision between 6pm and 2am: this will cover babysitting on domestic premises other than the child's home, e.g. at the neighbours' or friends' home and hotel babysitting services

- short-term occasional care where an individual child is looked after for less than two hours at a time, such as a supermarket crèche

- where the provision operates for six or fewer days on the same site. This will include mobile crèche companies who currently provide crèche facilities at short-term attractions

- activity-based provision including provision which includes mainly sporting activities, music, drama and dance activities, or art and craft activities. In all these cases childcare is incidental to the activity

- settings covered by the Adventure Activities Licensing Authority

- settings providing mainly religious education, such as Sunday schools and Madrassas etc.

Failure to register – childminders

If a childminder fails to a register, either as an early years childminder under s.33 or a later years childminder under s.52, then Ofsted can serve an 'enforcement notice' on the childminder. If a childminder continues to provide early years or later years childminding after the enforcement notice has been served then an offence is committed, and the childminder is liable on summary conviction to a fine of up to level 5 on the standard scale (£5000 in November 2006). An enforcement notice remains in place until Ofsted revokes it.

Exemption to registration – schools

There is an important additional exemption for other early years (s.34(2)) or later years (s.53(2)) provision. Provision for children aged 3 years and over that is provided by a maintained school, a non-maintained special school or an independent school is exempt from registration provided the provision is made by the school, and provided one or more registered pupils attend it. This means that much provision that previously was subject to a registration regime will not now have to register after the new arrangements come into place in September 2008.

However, schools will still have to register provision if:

- it is for children under three years

- it is made off-site where the site is not part of the school, for example a hall rented for the sole purpose of providing childcare

- the childcare that a school provides is not available to its own pupils

- a company not directly connected to the school makes provision on school premises.

The provision of childcare before and after school is pivotal to the Government's extended schools initiative. Further information is available in the DfES document *Planning and funding extended schools: a guide for local authorities and their partner organisations* (DfES, 2006j). The DfES document makes the following additional points.

- Where schools collaborate across a cluster of local schools to provide childcare and the care is located in one of the schools, there is no need for the provision to be registered by the 'host' school so long as some of that school's own pupils participate in the provision.

- Although registration is not compulsory for provision for children aged 8 and over, where schools make arrangements with third-party providers to make provision on school sites, the DfES will ask schools (using statutory guidance) to make arrangements only with those providers who have joined the Ofsted Childcare Register on a voluntary basis. This is because 'registration will signal to schools and parents that provision has met agreed requirements'.

Failure to register – other providers

It is an offence for a person to provide other non-exempt provision, either early years provision under s.34 or later years provision under s.53, without registering. The person is liable on summary conviction to a fine of up to level 5 on the standard scale (£5000 in November 2006). There is no provision for enforcement notices as there is for childminders, reflecting the very different nature of daycare provision from childminding. It is possible that a person could provide childminding in ignorance of the law. This is not the case with 'other' provision. See ss.87 and 88 on offences by corporate bodies and unincorporated associations.

Process of registration

The registration process for the two registers is very similar (see Table 5 for the relevant section of the Act). There are three distinct elements:

- application to register
- entry on register
- imposition of conditions on registration.

Table 5 Sections of the Act relating to the registration process

	Register	Provision	Registration requirements	Entry on register	Conditions on registration
Chapter 2 – early years	Early years register	childminding other	s.35 s.36	s.37	s.38
Chapter 3 – later years – required registration	Part A, General Childcare Register (Ofsted Childcare register)	childminding other	s.54 s.55	s.56	s.58
Chapter 4 – later years – voluntary registration	Part B, General Childcare Register (Ofsted Childcare register)	childminding other	s.62 s.63	s.64	s.66

In addition, ss.57 and 65 deal with registration on more than one register.

The application process – general

The application is made to Ofsted and must contain:

- prescribed information about prescribed matters

- other information reasonably required by Ofsted

- the prescribed fee (see s.89, page 109).

Prescribed requirements for registration

Sections 35, 36, 54, 55, 62 and 63 refer to 'the prescribed requirements for registration'. The Secretary of State is not constrained by the Act on the nature of the regulatory requirements that must be made by statutory instrument under s.105. Regulations can require information relating to:

- the applicant

- the premises on which the childcare is, or is to be, provided

- the arrangements for the childcare on those premises

- any person who may be caring for children on those premises
- any other person who may be on those premises.

Thus, regulations can specify qualifications of workers as well as their suitability in terms of child protection. The regulations can cover individuals not providing childcare, for example individuals living in the same premises as the domestic premises used by a childminder.

Ofsted will check each application against information held by the Criminal Records Bureau (CRB) and other sources. Part of the application process is to agree that third-party checks can be done on the applicant(s). If permission for these checks is refused by the applicant, Ofsted can turn down the application under s.90.

With application to both registers, Ofsted must grant the application if the prescribed requirements are satisfied and are likely to continue to be satisfied, and the applicant is not already disqualified under s.75. In all other cases, the application must be refused so that there is no room for doubt about the status of the application.

The first regulations for the compulsory registration arrangements are likely to be made by the Secretary of State around January 2008 in order to give sufficient time for providers to be registered by September 2008. Regulations for the voluntary part of the OCR are expected to be available in April 2007.

Information required by all applicants for the registers

The DfES paper *Childcare Bill: Part 3 – Childcare Regulations and Inspection Arrangements* (DfES, 2006d), gives the information that all applicants will have to provide. The regulations will not differ significantly from the current regulations: Child Minding and Day Care (Applications for Registration) (England) Regulations 2001 (SI 2001/1829) as amended by SI 2005/2296 (England. Statutory Instruments, 2005b). For all applicants this is likely to include:

- the applicant's full name and date of birth and, where the applicant is an organisation, details of the organisation and the individuals in charge. A distinction will be made between organisations where childcare is the primary purpose (in which case the details of all directors, trustees and others responsible for the management of the organisation will be required), and organisations where childcare provision is not the primary purpose (in which case only details of those with del-egated responsibility for the childcare will be required)

- the address and contact details (telephone number and email address, if avail-able) of the applicant, the address and other contact details for where the childcare is carried out, and whether or not those premises are domestic

- the proposed hours of operation, both in terms of the overall opening hours and the maximum length of time individual children will be looked after

- the proposed age range of the children to be looked after, with details of the num-bers of each age group, and with the applicant's own children, if any, separately identified

- details of the number of adults who will be looking after children

- details of the employment history, relevant experience and qualifications in respect of the applicant and person in charge

- details of criminal convictions or cautions relating to the applicant and person in charge.

See page 88 for DfES consultation document on the Ofsted Childcare Register.

Section 35: Applications for registration: early years childminders

See 'The application process – general', 'Information required by all applicants to the register' and 'Additional registration requirements for the Early Years Register'.

Additional registration requirements for the Early Years Register

The DfES paper *Childcare Bill: Part 3 – Childcare Regulations and Inspection Arrangements* (DfES, 2006d) gives further requirements for early years providers that are likely to form part of the 'prescribed requirements for registration'. Ofsted will require evidence that:

- the childminder or other provider is suitable to look after and be in regular con-tact with children

- the premises on which childcare is to be provided are suitable to be used for looking after children, having regard to their condition and the condition and appropriateness of any equipment on the premises and to any other factor connected with the situation, construction or size of the premises

- the applicant is judged to be able to meet the ongoing welfare, learning and development requirements in the Early Years Foundation Stage.

The last criterion will enable Ofsted to assess whether the childminder/provider is able to deliver both the welfare requirements, e.g. those relating to safeguarding children, and the learning and development requirements in the Early Years Foundation Stage. See ss.39 to 48.

Section 36: Applications for registration: other early years providers

In addition to the requirements in s.35, other provision will have to be registered in respect of particular premises. The 'prescribed requirements for registration' will take into account the different management arrangements. The DfES paper states that the regulation making powers will be used to ensure the registering person (this includes individuals, corporate bodies or unincorporated associations) and the person in day-to-day charge of the provision are suitable to look after and be in regular contact with children. In each case of a corporate body or an unincorporated association providing childcare, Ofsted will decide in the circumstances how suitability is judged. It may mean that an individual who is a board member of the body providing childcare will be assessed for suitability even though he or she does not provide childcare directly. CRB disclosures will be required for each person on whom details have been supplied as helping to provide childcare.

Section 37: Entry on the register and certificates

There are separate sections dealing with registration certificates for the three registers:

- s.37 for early years providers registering on the Early Years Register

- s.56 for later years providers where a registration is required (compulsory part of the OCR)

- s.64 for voluntary registration (voluntary part of the OCR).

In addition, s.92 deals with combined registration certificates, that is, for example, certificates where a provider provides both early years and later years childminding, and is dealt with under that section.

The law on certificates is the same for each type of registration.

Once an application is successful, Ofsted must place the person on the relevant register and issue a certificate of registration. For 'other' providers, i.e. providers who are not childminders, the registration must be in respect of particular premises. The *Explanatory Notes* to the Act observe: 'This means that ... providers (other than childminders) may have separate entries in the register in respect of different premises (where they provide childcare at more than one location).' However, see s.94 (page 112) for the possibility of a single registration covering more than one site.

In addition, the law requires the certificate of registration to set out particular information, as prescribed through regulations. DfES *Childcare Bill: Part 3 – Childcare Regulations and Inspection Arrangements* (DfES, 2006d) states that the regulations will be similar to the existing regulations Child Minding and Day Care (Certificates of Registration) (England) Regulations 2001 (SI 2001/1830) (England. Statutory Instruments, 2001) with amendments to take account of the new registration arrangements. The required information is, therefore:

• the name of the registered person
• the address at which childcare is provided, although this is not required for childminders as their activity is not confined in the same way to one set of premises
• which register(s) the provider is registered on
• any conditions applicable to the registration (see s.38).

The current regulations also require childcare providers (not childminders) to display their registration certificates and this will continue.

Finally, Ofsted can:

• amend a registration certificate if there is a change of circumstance
• issue a copy of a certificate, on payment of a fee as required by regulations (£5 in October 2006), if the original certificate has been lost or destroyed.

Section 38: Conditions on registration

Ofsted may impose conditions on providers to specify particular requirements relating to individual childcare settings that it would not be possible to specify in general requirements that apply to all settings. The conditions are specified as part of the registration process. The law is the same for the three registers:

- s.38 for early years providers for the Early Years Register
- s.58 for the compulsory OCR
- s.66 for the voluntary OCR.

In addition, for early years providers, Ofsted can make a specific condition to comply with the Early Years Foundation Stage or any part of it.

Ofsted can impose any condition thought appropriate, and any condition can be varied or removed at any time. Examples of conditions given by the DfES in the *Childcare Bill: Part 3 – Childcare Regulations and Inspection Arrangements* (DfES, 2006d) include the number of children that a provider is permitted to look after, or restrictions on the use of parts of the premises where these are unsafe for children.

A person commits an offence if he or she does not comply with a condition, and is liable on summary conviction to a fine of up to level 5 on the standard scale (£5000 in November 2006).

Requirements to be met by early years providers

Sections 39 to 46 set out the requirements relating to the Early Years Foundation Stage (EYFS) which must be met, and continue to be met, by early years providers.

Section 39: The Early Years Foundation Stage

The EYFS is a single quality framework for care, development and learning for children from birth to 5. The Government gave a commitment to produce the EYFS in *Choice for parents, the best start for children: a ten year strategy for childcare* (HM Treasury *et al.*, 2004). The EYFS largely consists of the existing three frameworks:

- *Birth to Three Matters Framework* (2003)

- *Curriculum Guidance for the Foundation Stage* (2000)

- *National Standards for Under Eights' Day Care and Childminding* (2003).

Section 39 requires the EYFS to consist of two parts:

- learning and development requirements

- welfare requirements.

See s.41 for more information on the learning and development requirements. The Secretary of State can by order under s.39(1) use a statutory instrument (see ss.104 and 105) to establish the learning and development requirements. Section 41(6) calls such an order 'a learning and development order'. The order is likely under s.44 to specify a document that contains the detailed learning and development requirements. Regulations under s.43 enable the Secretary of State to set out the welfare requirements in regulations.

Consultation on proposals for the EYFS closed on 28 July 2006. See the DfES and DWP document *The Early Years Foundation Stage: consultation on a single quality framework for services to children from birth to five* (DfES and DWP, 2006b). The final framework is expected in early 2007, with the implementation of the framework as mandatory for all registered early years providers from September 2008.

Section 40: Duty to implement Early Years Foundation Stage

The duty to implement both parts of the EYFS (learning and development requirements, and welfare requirements) falls on all early years providers who are registered with Ofsted, i.e. the EYFS is for all children attending registered early years provision. A child can participate in early years provision from birth until 31 August after the child's fifth birthday. See ss.33 and 34.

The duty also applies to providers of early years education for over threes in maintained schools, approved non-maintained special schools and independent schools, even though such providers are exempted from the duty to register on the Early Years Register. See 'Exemption to registration – schools' on page 66.

Section 68 states that a person's registration on the Early Years Register can be cancelled if the duty to implement the EYFS is not met.

Section 41: Learning and development requirements

Six areas of learning and development (s.41(3)) underpin the learning and development requirements. They are:

- personal, social and emotional development
- communication, language and literacy
- problem solving, reasoning and numeracy
- knowledge and understanding of the world
- physical development
- creative development.

The six areas are the same as those in the *Curriculum Guidance for the Foundation Stage* (QCA and DfEE, 2000), which was put into legislation by s.83 (Curriculum requirements for the foundation stage) of the Education Act 2002. The only difference is that 'problem solving, reasoning and numeracy' is substituted for 'mathematical development'.

The areas of learning and development may be amended by an order of the Secretary of State under s.41(4) but an affirmative order is required (see s.105).

For each area of learning and development, early learning goals, educational programmes and assessment arrangements may be specified under s.41(2). This replaces the provision in s.87(2) of the Education Act 2002.

Under s.41(5), a learning and development order cannot require:

- the allocation of any particular period or periods of time to the teaching of any educational programme or any matter, skill or process forming part of it
- the making in the timetables of any early years provider of provision of any particular kind for the periods to be allocated to such teaching.

This replaces the provision in s.87(4) of the Education Act 2002.

Early learning goals

The early learning goals are defined in s.41(2)(a) as 'The knowledge, skills and understanding which young children of different abilities and maturities are expected to have before the 1st September next following the day on which they attain the age of five'.

The early learning goals provide guidance to practitioners about the levels of understanding, skills and knowledge that young children are anticipated to have between the ages of 3 and 5. The early learning goals and Foundation Stage profile (the observational assessment of the early learning goals) replaced baseline testing in 2002. The existing early learning goals are not lost in the development of this new framework. The consultation document on the EYFS highlights the early learning goals for each area of learning and development.

The QCA consulted in May to July 2006 on a proposal, in advance of the final EYFS document being published. One early learning goal was amended from 'Hear and say initial and final sounds in words, and short vowel sounds within words' to 'Hear and say sounds in words in the order in which they occur'. The implementation of this new early learning goal is expected to be from September 2006 and is as a result of the recommendations from the Rose Review of the teaching of early reading into teaching reading (2006):

> *The forthcoming Early Years Foundation Stage and the renewed Primary National Strategy Framework for teaching literacy should provide, as a priority, clear guidance on developing children's speaking and listening skills ... the Early Years Foundation Stage and the renewed literacy framework must be compatible with each other and make sure that expectations about continuity and progression in phonic work are expressed explicitly in the new guidance.*
> Independent review of the teaching of early reading, Final Report, Jim Rose, March 2006, recommendations, page 73

Educational programmes – the 'taught' debate

The 'educational programmes' are defined in s.41(2)(b) as 'the matters, skills and processes which are required to be taught to young children of different abilities and maturities'.

There was much debate in Parliament about the word 'taught'. Concern centred around the interpretation of the meaning of 'taught' by practitioners, and the fear of a framework that would encourage the formal teaching of children from birth to 5. The government Minister, Lord Adonis, responded to these concerns with reference to the glossary to the *Early Years Foundation Stage* consultation document (DfES and DWP, 2006a), which states that:

> *Teaching has many aspects, including planning and creating a learning environment, organising time and material resources, interacting, questioning, responding to questions, working with and observing children, assessing and recording children's progress, and sharing knowledge gained with other practitioners and parents.*

He noted that 'most people, and certainly most early years practitioners, would recognise this as teaching, although it is both age-appropriate and informal' (Hansard, HL, 2006e, c338).

The EYFS consultation document (page 16) states that 'play underpins all development and learning for young children' (DfES and DWP, 2006a). This was confirmed by the Minister for Children, Young People and Families in a speech during the Commons Standing Committee debates:

> *... the Early Years Foundation Stage will cover the wide range of processes, planning and teaching needed by practitioners to provide an effective, stimulating, play-based environment to enable young children to learn and develop at their own pace – a pace that is appropriate to their age and ability. That includes practitioners establishing relationships with babies and young children, and their parents; planning the learning environment; supporting and extending children's play, learning and development; and observing and assessing children's achievements; and planning for each child's next steps. That is far from the formal education that I believe is in Members' minds when they think of the word 'taught'.*
> Beverley Hughes MP, Hansard. HC, 2005d, Standing Committee D, c251

Assessment arrangements

The 'assessment arrangements' are defined in s.41(2)(c) as 'the arrangements which are required for assessing children for the purpose of ascertaining what they have achieved in relation to the early learning goals'.

Lord Adonis made the following statement of reassurance about the assessment arrangements.

The Early Years Foundation Stage will require those who plan and deliver early years provision to assess children through ongoing observation through the normal course of a child's learning and play. There will be no testing during this important stage of children's learning and development. However, the term 'assessment' also incorporates the observations and contributions made by parents and other early years settings to inform a profile of the whole child. To say in the Bill that assessment has to be undertaken by observation would narrow the interpretation and not reflect the valuable contribution made by parents and other settings to a child's overall assessments.
Hansard. HL, 2006f, c.340

The assessment arrangements – currently known as the Foundation Stage Profile – will be renamed the Early Years Foundation Stage Profile but will serve the same function and be subject to minor changes reflected in the development of the EYFS.

Section 42: Further provisions about assessment arrangements

In order to support the assessment arrangements for the EYFS, the Secretary of State can use a learning and development order (see s.39) to confer or impose functions on:

- an early years provider

- the governing body or headteacher of a maintained school

- a local authority.

The order may specify details of how, when and by whom young children are to be assessed under the EYFS.

Provision must be made for establishing whether the aim of the assessment arrangements is being achieved. To aid this, providers including schools may be required to allow anyone to whom the order has granted responsibility to monitor assessment arrangements to enter premises and monitor those arrangements.

An order specifying assessment arrangements may be published in a separate document.

This section replaces s.87(6) and (8) to (11) of the Education Act 2002.

Section 43: Welfare requirements

The purpose of the welfare requirements as set out in the Explanatory Notes is to:

• secure young children's safety and welfare when they are in early years provision

• ensure effective organisation of an early years setting

• set out procedures for dealing with complaints and the provision of information.

The Secretary of State has wide powers to make regulations – to be known as the 'Welfare Regulations' – to achieve these objectives for all early years providers. The Act gives a list of the issues that may be regulated, but it is not exclusive:

• the welfare of the children concerned

• the arrangements for safeguarding the children concerned

• suitability of persons to care for, or be in regular contact with, the children concerned

• qualifications and training

• the suitability of premises and equipment

• the manner in which the early years provision is organised

• procedures for dealing with complaints

• the keeping of records

• the provision of information.

The list replaces the one found in s.79C of the Children Act 1989 and the 'Welfare Regulations' will replace The Day Care and Child Minding (National Standards) (England) Regulations 2003 (SI 2003/1996) (England. Statutory Instruments, 2003b) as amended by SI 2005/2303. The *National Standards for Under Eights' Daycare and Childminding* (2003) will be replaced by the Early Years Foundation Stage framework. Thus standard 4.11 for outdoor play areas changes in the EYFS consultation document (page 125) from:

Normally, outdoor play space adjoining the premises is provided. It is safe, secure and well maintained. Exceptionally, where outdoor play space cannot be provided, children are safely escorted to local parks, playgrounds or the equivalent on a regular basis.

to:

Wherever possible, there is access to an outdoor play area. Where outdoor play space cannot be provided, outings are planned to local parks or playgrounds on a daily basis.

Before making welfare regulations, the Secretary of State must consult Ofsted and any other persons he or she considers appropriate. Except where a new regulation has to be made urgently, a draft of the regulations will be issued for public consultation. The welfare regulations may include that a person who fails to comply with any requirement of the regulations (without a reasonable excuse) can be found guilty of an offence and fined up to level 5 on the standard scale (£5000 in November 2006).

Section 44: Instruments specifying learning and development or welfare requirements

This section enables a 'learning and development order' or the 'welfare regulations' to refer to another document. This is a standard procedure that enabled the *Curriculum Guidance for the Foundation Stage* (2000) and *National Standards for Under Eights' Day Care and Childminding* (2003) to be given a statutory basis.

A 'learning and development order' or the 'welfare regulations' can also confer powers and impose duties on Ofsted in the exercise of its functions under Part 3 of the Act. For example, Ofsted could be asked to have regard to advice or guidance from the National Assessment Agency.

Under Part 3, in the event of any actions or legal proceedings, Ofsted can take into account the fact that an early years provider or a school governing body (or headteacher) has failed to meet any of the provisions of a 'learning and development order' or the 'welfare regulations' or any document referred to in the instruments. For example, this enables Ofsted to use the failure to meet a welfare standard set out in the Early Years Foundation Stage as the grounds for disqualifying an early years provider from the register.

Section 45: Procedure for making certain orders

Before making, or amending, a learning and development order the Secretary of State must consult appropriate bodies representing early years providers about the proposal. The draft order will then be published, along with a summary of representative views to enable all those with a special interest in the EYFS to make any further representations over a one-month period. The Secretary of State has the power to make the changes with or without modifications. This replaces the current provision in s.96 of the Education Act 2002.

Section 46: Power to enable exemptions to be conferred

The intention behind the establishment of the EYFS is that all children regardless of the setting they attend will receive high-quality integrated care and education. However, s.46 sets out the circumstances in which exemptions to the delivery of the EYFS can apply. It is intended that the power to enable exemptions will only be used in exceptional circumstances and refer to the learning and development requirements only.

Section 46 enables the Secretary of State to issue exemptions in two ways:

- in prescribed circumstances to an early years provider or class of early years providers

- in prescribed circumstances in relation to a particular young child.

A particular early years provider or a particular category of early years provider can be exempt from delivering some or all of the EYFS. Further details will be explained in forthcoming regulations.

This provision was made in order to accommodate some providers who are currently exempt under the Curriculum Guidance for the Foundation Stage. Some early years providers may not be able to meet the full EYFS standards by September 2008, so a time-limited exemption would prevent the provision being closed. The Minster (Lord Adonis) envisaged that:

exemptions or modifications in respect of providers should be made only in exceptional circumstances for a limited period (no longer than 6 months) to

allow them time to improve their standards in order to meet the full requirements. During the period of such an exemption or modification, local authorities would be expected to use their powers under s.13 to support providers in improving the quality of provision. Supporting existing providers to improve will be a key priority for local authorities in advance of the full implementation of the EYFS in two years' time.
Hansard. HL, 2006g, c342

However, Lord Adonis agreed that any new provision setting up after April 2008 would not be exempt from delivering the EYFS.

The second circumstance for an exemption applies to individual children. Regulations may enable an early years provider to determine whether a particular young child should not be supported through the EYFS, or some elements of it. Concerns were raised about the onus on the provider to make such decisions and ministers confirmed that this provision is to allow parents to make the choice for their child not to be included in the EYFS, for example, because of religious beliefs. This also ensures parents' rights under the European Convention on Human Rights that their children are educated in accordance with their own philosophies and beliefs.

Further reassurances were given about young disabled children and children with English as a second language or special education needs. It is the intention that the EYFS is fully inclusive and therefore these will not be reasons for children to be exempt from receiving the EYFS (see Lords Hansard. HL, 2006h, c343).

Section 47: Independent schools

Section 157 (Independent school standards) of the Education Act 2002 is amended to require independent schools to use the EYFS as part of the independent school standards. In addition, independent schools providing for pupils before their third birthday must register as an early years provider (in the same way that an LA-maintained school must do).

Section 48 and Schedule 1: Amendments relating to curriculum

Schedule 1 amends the law on the National Curriculum for England in the Education Act 2002 in order to introduce the Early Years Foundation Stage. All references to the Foundation Stage (as part of the National Curriculum) are removed. The only requirement remaining in the 2002 Act that applies to under fives is that the curriculum for all registered pupils at LA-maintained schools, including LA-maintained nursery schools, must comply with the 'General Requirements', namely that a school's curriculum must be a balanced and broadly based curriculum that:

- promotes the spiritual, moral, cultural, mental and physical development of pupils at the school and of society

- prepares pupils at the school for the opportunities, responsibilities and experiences of later life.

Schedule 1 amends the functions of the Qualification and Curriculum Authority (QCA) contained in the Education Act 1997. Responsibility for 'funded nursery education' (the statutory term for 'free' nursery education provided mainly in the private and voluntary sector, that is (in 2006) the 12.5 hours a week for 38 weeks) is removed from the QCA.

The Secretary of State is given the power by order (see s.104), after consulting the QCA, to confer additional functions on the QCA over 'young children' (see s.19) in LA-maintained schools and those for whom early years provision (see s.40) is made. The QCA was formally involved in the development of the Early Years Foundation Stage as members of the steering group who oversaw its development and as stakeholders at the consultation meeting. Most of the development work has been undertaken by the DfES and the Primary National Strategy. The National Assessment Agency based in the QCA has had a role in the development of the Early Years Foundation Stage profile. The Secretary of State will have to make an order to allow this work to continue once Schedule 1 commences.

Inspection

The inspection arrangements in ss.49 and 50 replace the existing two inspection and reporting regimes for early years provision covering:

- nursery education (in Schedule 26 of the School Standards and Framework Act 1998)

- childcare (in s.79Q and 79R of the Children Act 1989).

The respective regulations, the Nursery Education (Inspection) (England) Regulations 2005 (SI 2005/2299) (England. Statutory Instruments, 2005e) and the Day Care and Child Minding (Inspection) (England) Regulations 2005 (SI 2005/2300) (England. Statutory Instruments, 2005a), will also be replaced.

The DfES *Childcare Bill: Part 3 – Childcare Regulations and Inspection Arrangements* (DfES, 2006d) paper commits Ofsted to maintaining the current three-year inspection cycle (a matter for regulations under the Act). The paper goes on to record that:

> *Ofsted will develop and consult on a new inspection framework that will cover early years provision and on separate arrangements for inspection of later years provision. They will be looking to develop a proportionate approach, particularly for the elements of later years provision which are not currently subject to inspection. We need to balance different objectives. Our priority is for a regime that safeguards children, and encourages childcare providers to give them a high quality environment and experience in their setting. On the other hand, we do not want a system in which Ofsted is obliged to monitor too frequently or intensively those providers who are offering high quality childcare, and with whom parents have no complaints.*
> DfES (2006d)

See also s.60 on inspection of later years provision for persons registered under the compulsory part of the OCR. There is no provision for regular inspection of provision made by persons registered under the voluntary part of the OCR although Ofsted does have the power to enter the premises used by a person on the voluntary register (see s.77).

Section 49: Inspections

Ofsted must inspect early years providers at:

- intervals (to be prescribed in regulations, but likely to be three years)
- the request from the Secretary of State (and the request can be to inspect provision at a particular address or a set of premises).

Ofsted may inspect an early years provider at any other time when it is considered appropriate.

Ofsted can treat the findings of an inspection requested by the Secretary of State or one done using Ofsted's discretionary power to inspect when it considers it appropriate as an inspection done as part the regular cycle of inspections.

In addition, regulations made under s.49 may:

- set out the circumstances where Ofsted is not required to carry out a regular inspection when it falls due – the DfES gives the example of when there are no children on roll

- allow Ofsted not to inspect an independent school where a body approved by the Secretary of State undertakes inspections – this mirrors the current arrangement that the Independent Schools Inspectorate inspects schools in membership of a body (Head Master's Conference, Girl's School Association, etc) affiliated to the Independent Schools Council

- require the registered person to notify particular people of an inspection – parents are told under the Day Care and Child Minding (Inspection) (England) Regulations 2005 (SI 2005/2300) (England. Statutory Instruments, 2005a) and the local authority is told under the Nursery Education (Inspection) (England) Regulations 2005 (SI 2005/2299) (England. Statutory Instruments, 2005e).

See also s.77 for the authorisation of inspectors to carry out this work and the rights of entry to premises.

Section 50: Report of inspections

This section and s.61, which relates to inspection of later years provision, are the same except that Ofsted must publish a report of an early years inspection. For a later years inspection, Ofsted may publish if it wishes, although the likelihood is that all such reports will be published.

Reports have to set out Ofsted's findings on:

- the contribution of the provision to the well-being of children

- the quality and standards of provision

- how well the provision meets the needs of the range of children receiving provision

- the quality of leadership and management of the provision.

See s.31 for how this feeds into Ofsted's annual report and its repeal by the Education and Inspections (E&I) Act. The E&I Act also repeals subsection (4) in both ss.5 and 6. Subsection (4) allows Ofsted to publish reports by electronic means and for reports to be exempt from legal action on the grounds of defamation unless they can be shown to have been made with malice. The E&I Act contains new provisions on both these issues.

Ofsted must send a report to the Secretary of State if requested, and ensure the registered person receives a copy. Ofsted can publish the report in any convenient manner, but must send the report to other persons, if required by regulations. A fee can be charged. The existing regulations (see s.49) require Ofsted to send a copy to parents and the local authority. For a nursery education inspection at an independent school, the headteacher must also receive a copy.

Section 51: Interpretation of Chapter 2

This section lists the statutory references for those terms used in the Early Years Foundation Stage.

Part 3, Chapter 3: Regulation of Later Years Provision for children under 8

This chapter (ss.52 to 61) sets out the registration and inspection requirements on later years providers who have to register on the compulsory part of the Ofsted Childcare Register (OCR).

Later years provision is defined in s.96(6) as childcare provision beginning with the 1 September after a child's fifth birthday and ending on a day to be prescribed by order of the Secretary of State. However, ss.52(1) and 53(1) limit compulsory registration by providers to provision for children who have not attained the age of 8. Childcare is defined in s.18 as education and any other supervised activity.

Sections 52 and 53 state who should be registered on the compulsory OCR, and ss.54 to 57 set out how a person registers on the compulsory OCR. Section 58 specifies the conditions that can be put on registration and s.59 the regulations governing activities. Sections 60 and 61 deal with Ofsted inspection of provision and the publication of reports.

Many of the provisions of this chapter mirror those for early years providers in Chapter 2 of the Act. Rather than repeating material, the differences in registration procedures are explained where appropriate.

Section 52: Requirement to register – later years childminders for children under 8

A person cannot provide later years childminding for children up to the age of 8 unless he or she is registered on the compulsory part of the OCR.

Later years childminding is defined in s.94 as later years provision on domestic premises for reward. If at any time the number of adults caring for children exceeds three then the provision has to be registered as 'other' later years provision under s.53.

For exemptions to registration, see notes under s.33 (page 65) and for exemptions to registration – schools see notes under s.34 (page 66).

For information about the failure to register childminders, see notes under s.33 (page 66) and for the failure to register other providers see notes under s.34 (page 67).

Section 53: Requirement to register: other later years providers for children under 8

For 'other' later years provision, i.e. provision that is not childminding, the registration is in respect of particular premises, and the person in charge has to register the provision. The person in charge can be an individual, two or more individuals acting as an unincorporated association, or a corporate body be it a charity or a company. See s.94 for a power that the Secretary of State has to amend legislation so that a person (most likely a corporate body) only has to make one registration when provision is made at multiple premises. See also the notes on exemptions to registration under ss.33 and 34. LA-maintained and independent schools are exempt from the need to register.

For a description of the registration process, see page 67.

Section 54: Applications for registration – later years childminders

Applications are made to Ofsted and must contain:

• prescribed information about prescribed matters

• other information reasonably required by Ofsted

• the prescribed fee.

See page 68 for the prescribed requirements for registration and page 69 for information required by all applicants for the register.

The DfES *Ofsted Childcare Register – Consultation Paper* (DfES and DWP, 2006c) gives further information about DfES thinking on how the OCR will operate. The consultation paper distinguishes between registration requirements that applicants must attain to achieve registration and requirements that govern activity, which covers activities that will not necessarily be in place at the time of registration, particularly for new providers, e.g. staff may not have all been recruited. The paper divides these into requirements relating to people, premises and provision. Thus, for example, the registering person must provide evidence of a relevant and valid first aid qualification. See below for conditions on registration (ss.58 and 66), and regulations governing activities (ss. 59 and 67).

Section 55: Applications for registration – other later years providers

As with early years provision, an application to register later years provision that is not childminding must be for provision at a specified address. See also s.54.

Section 56: Entry on the register and certificates

See s.37 (page 77).

Section 57: Special procedure for registered early years providers

If a registered early years provider requests to be placed on the compulsory part of the OCR, Ofsted must comply with the request and issue a certificate. Note that an early years childminder can only request to go on the compulsory OCR as a childminder. For non-childminding provision, the provision must be at the same premises as the early years provision otherwise a separate registration is required.

The DfES consultation paper *Ofsted Childcare Register* (DfES and DWP, 2006c) states (para.25) that the requirements for a person to be registered on the Early Years Register will be so framed that the person can be automatically registered on both parts of the OCR. There will be no need to go through a separate application process or pay a separate or additional fee.

The same rules apply about amendments to registration certificates and their replacement if lost or destroyed. See s.37 (page 71) and s.65 (page 95).

Section 58: Conditions on registration

See s.38 (page 73).

Section 59: Regulations governing activities

This section has the same purpose as s.43 (Welfare requirements) has for early years provision, namely to set out the expected standards for the welfare and safety of children under 8 participating in later years provision, along with standards for the qualifications of staff, complaints and the keeping of records.

The section contains the same non-exclusive list of areas where the Secretary of State has power to regulate provision as in section 43, namely:

- the welfare of the children concerned

- the arrangements for safeguarding the children concerned

- suitability of persons to care for, or be in regular contact with, the children concerned

- qualifications and training

- the suitability of premises and equipment

- the manner in which the early years provision is organised

- procedures for dealing with complaints

- the keeping of records

- the provision of information.

The Government has not indicated how much of The Day Care and Child Minding (National Standards) (England) Regulations 2003 (SI 2003/1996) (England. Statutory Instruments, 2003b) as amended by SI 2005/2303 (England. Statutory Instruments, 2005c) and the *National Standards for Under Eights' Daycare and Childminding* (2003) will be used for the standards for later years provisions under this section.

The regulations can impose duties on Ofsted in its registration and inspection work under Part 3 of the Act, including requirements on Ofsted to have regard to welfare standards in the regulations or specified documents. Non-compliance with such standards can be used by Ofsted to disqualify a provider or, in certain cases, may make the provider guilty of an offence that, on summary conviction, may result in a fine up to level 5 on the standard scale (£5000 in November 2006).

Inspection

The inspection arrangements in ss.60 and 61 replace the existing inspection and reporting regime found in s.79Q and 79R of the Children Act 1989 and the Day Care and Child Minding (Inspection) (England) Regulations 2005 (SI 2005/2300) (England. Statutory Instruments, 2005a). See the introduction to inspection for early years provision (page 83).

Section 60: Inspections

The regulations cannot specify a mandatory inspection cycle for the later years inspections. Thus Ofsted:

- must inspect later years providers at the request from the Secretary of State (and the request can be to inspect provision at a particular address or a set of premises)

- may inspect a later years provider at any other time when it is considered appropriate.

In addition, regulations may require the registered person to notify particular people of an inspection, for example parents and the LA.

Section 61: Report of inspections

There is no requirement to publish a report of a later years inspection under this Chapter. See notes under s.50 (page 83).

Part 3, Chapter 4: Voluntary registration

This Chapter (ss.62 to 67) deals with registration on the voluntary part of the Ofsted Childcare Register (OCR). The voluntary OCR is open to persons who provide one or more of the following:

- early years childcare that is exempt from the Early Years Register (EYR)

- later years childcare that, although provision is made for 6- and 7-year-olds, is exempt from the compulsory part of the OCR

- later years childcare for children aged 8 years and over.

However, schools that provide childcare which is exempt from the EYR or compulsory OCR cannot join the voluntary OCR.

The principal reasons for joining the register are that registration:

- allows providers to demonstrate a commitment to a minimum quality standard

- enables information about the provision to be automatically available from the local authority's Children's Information Service (see s.12)

- allows providers to work with schools as schools will be given statutory guidance to contract only with childcare providers who are on the voluntary register for children aged eight years or over

- provides parents with access to financial support through the Working Tax Credit or employer-supported childcare vouchers.

Providers who are exempt from registration on the EYR and compulsory OCR

Providers who are exempt from the requirement to register on the EYRs or the compulsory part of the OCR may wish to register on the voluntary part of the OCR. This is likely to cover nannies in domestic premises and providers who put on crèches at sporting events, etc (see 'Exemptions to registration' on page 65). Although provision in schools for children over three is exempt, s.63(3) prevents schools from registering voluntarily. Local authorities are not prevented from registering youth service provision or other leisure-time or sporting activity.

Provision for children aged 8 years and over

Registration is voluntary on the OCR for childcare providers, including childminding that is for children aged 8 and over. However, see 'Exemption to registration – schools' on page 66: the DfES will ask schools to arrange childcare for children aged 8 and over with third-party providers who have registered on the voluntary part of the OCR. This is because 'registration will signal to schools and parents that provision has met agreed requirements' (DfES, 2006g).

Upper age limit of 'later years provision'

In order to register, the childcare will have to come within the definition of 'later years provision', the upper age limit of which will be prescribed in regulations by the Secretary of State under s.96(6)(b). The maximum possible age is 17 years, that is up to a child's 18th birthday (see the definition of a child in s.106). The Regulatory Impact Assessment to the DfES Consultation Paper on the *Ofsted Childcare Register* (DfES and DWP, 2006c) (see page 88) suggests in paragraph 4 that the upper limit will be set at 14 years (or 18 years if the child is disabled). The duty to secure sufficient childcare provision in s.6 applied up to a child's 14th birthday (and 18th if the child is disabled).

Nature of voluntary registration and termination

Voluntary registration is not a qualification; like the other registrations, it is a 'licence' to provide childcare, although not a mandatory licence. Registration has to be in relation to actual provision that the applicant intends to make. Also, s.68 (Cancellation of registration) enables Ofsted to cancel a childminder's registration if it appears that the person has not childminded for a period of more than three years. Section 71 (Termination of voluntary registration on expiry of prescribed period) allows the Secretary of State to prescribe a period after which voluntary registration will expire.

The registration process is similar in many respects to the two other registration processes. The main difference is that childcare is not inspected by Ofsted even though an application for registration has to be with a view to making, or continuing to make, provision. Section 77 does, though, give a right to authorised Ofsted inspectors to inspect premises where someone on the voluntary OCR register is providing childcare.

Section 62: Applications for registration on the general register – childminders

A person who provides childminding for children aged 8 years and over, or is otherwise exempt ('Exemptions to registration' on page 65), may apply to be registered on the voluntary OCR register.

Applications are made to Ofsted and must contain:

* prescribed information about prescribed matters

* other information reasonably required by Ofsted

* the prescribed fee.

See page 68 for the 'Prescribed requirements for registration' and page 69 for 'Information required by all applicants for the register'. See s.54 for information about the DfES *Ofsted Childcare Register – Consultation Paper* (DfES and DWP, 2006c).

Section 63: Applications for registration on the general register – other childcare providers

A person who provides childcare (other than a childminder) who is not required to register on the EYR or the compulsory OCR may register on the voluntary OCR (see s.62). As with the EYR and compulsory registration on the OCR, an application to register on the voluntary OCR, which is not for childminding, must be for provision at a specified set of premises. However, s.63(3) stops childcare made directly by a school from registering on the voluntary OCR.

Section 64: Entry on the register and certificates

See s.37.

Section 65: Special procedure for persons already registered

If a registered early years or later years provider (that is someone who is registered on the EYR or the compulsory OCR) requests to be placed on the voluntary OCR, Ofsted must comply with the request and issue a certificate.

Note that a childminder can only request to go on the voluntary OCR as a childminder. For non-childminding provision, the provider must make provision at the same set of premises as that registered on the EYR or the compulsory OCR.

The DfES consultation paper *Ofsted Childcare Register*, paragraph 25 (DfES and DWP, 2006c) states that the requirements for a person to be registered on the EYR will be so framed that the person can be automatically registered on both parts of the OCR. There will be no need to go through a separate application process or pay a separate or additional fee.

The same rules apply about amendments to registration certificates and their replacement if lost or destroyed (see s.37 and s.57).

Section 66: Conditions on registration

See s.38.

Section 67: Regulations governing activities

This section applies to persons who have registered voluntarily on the OCR because they are providing early or later years provision but are not required to be registered on the EYR or the compulsory part of the OCR.

This section has the same purpose as s.43 (Welfare requirements) has for early years provision and s.59 (Regulations governing activities) has for later years provision for children under 8. The section enables the Secretary of State to set out in regulations the expected standards for the welfare and safety of children participating in provision made by people registered on the voluntary OCR, along with standards for the qualifications of staff, complaints and the keeping of records.

The section contains the same non-exclusive list of areas where the Secretary of State has power to regulate provision as in ss.43 and 59, namely:

- the welfare of the children concerned
- the arrangements for safeguarding the children concerned
- suitability of persons to care for, or be in regular contact with, the children concerned
- qualifications and training
- the suitability of premises and equipment
- the manner in which the early years provision is organised
- procedures for dealing with complaints
- the keeping of records
- the provision of information.

The regulations can impose duties on Ofsted in its registration and inspection work under Part 3 of the Act, including requirements on Ofsted to have regard to welfare standards in the regulations or specified documents. Non-compliance with such standards can be used by Ofsted to disqualify a provider. As registration is voluntary, non-compliance is not a criminal offence.

Part 3, Chapter 5: Common provisions

Chapters 2, 3 and 4 dealt with the separate arrangements for registration, requirements governing activities and inspection of early years providers, later years providers for under eights, and the voluntary registration for other childcare providers. Chapter 5 (ss.68 to 98) sets out requirements that are common to all three types of registration. These provisions in most cases rely heavily on the current requirements for childminding and daycare found in Part 10A of the Children Act 1989 as amended.

While the arrangements for registering are separate, the law on removal of registration is the same for the Early Years Register (EYR) and the Ofsted Childcare Register (OCR).

Section 68: Cancellation of registration

Ofsted can cancel a provider's registration if the provider:

- no longer satisfies the registration requirements (see ss.35, 36, 54, 55, 62 and 63)

- has not complied with a condition imposed on registration (see ss.38, 58 and 66)

- has not complied with a requirement imposed by regulations, for example the welfare regulations (see ss. 43, 59 and 67)

- has not implemented successfully the EYFS under s.40 (for an early years provider)

- has not paid the registration fee under s.89 (see below).

However, Ofsted cannot cancel a provider's registration if the time given at registration to complete improvements (called 'changes or additions' in the Act) to services, equipment or premises has not expired, although registration can still be cancelled for other unrelated reasons, for example non payment of registration fees.

In addition, Ofsted can cancel a childminder's registration if the childminder appears not to have childminded for three years while registered.

Section 69: Suspension of registration

The Chief Inspector can suspend a person's registration. Further details will be set out in regulations. The DfES paper *Childcare Bill: Part 3 – Childcare Regulation and Inspection Arrangements,* paragraph 20 (DfES, 2006d) states that regulations will be used to suspend a person's registration where there are concerns about children being exposed to risk of harm:

> *The purpose of the suspension would be to allow Ofsted to investigate such concerns and/or to allow time for steps to be taken to eliminate the risk.*

The DfES paper indicates that the Child Minding and Day Care (Suspension of Registration) (England) Regulations 2003 (England. Statutory Instruments, 2003a) would be followed:

> *We propose that the initial period of suspension is 6 weeks, but this would be able to be extended for up to 12 weeks and, exceptionally, for a longer period, for example to allow for completion of a lengthy police investigation. The regulations would specify the arrangements for lifting the suspension, once Ofsted is satisfied that the grounds for the suspension no longer apply, and for Ofsted's formal notifications to the provider of the suspension, which would include the reasons for the decision, and of any decision to lift the suspension. Under the regulations, a provider would be able to exercise a right of appeal to the relevant independent tribunal against any suspension decision by Ofsted.*

The right of appeal will be to the Care Standards Tribunal (CST) against a suspension. See www.carestandardstribunal.gov.uk/ for more information on the work of the Tribunal.

An offence may be committed if a person continues to work while suspended, and on summary conviction can lead to a fine not exceeding level 5 on the standard scale (£5000 in November 2006). No offence is committed if a person continues to work (or begins to work elsewhere) in childcare if registration is not required, for example childcare for children over 3 that is part of a school's directly provided extended school activities, although a school might wish to ask potential employees whether they are suspended. If the concern is about a child protection matter the enhanced criminal record check should provide this information.

It is also not an offence for a person who has been suspended from one register to continue to work as a registered childcare worker where the registration has not been suspended. Thus, an early years childminder who is suspended from the EYR but is also registered in, but not suspended from, the compulsory part of the OCR can continue to work as a later years childminder. The likelihood is that if the reasons for suspension were sufficiently serious, Ofsted would suspend a provider from all the registers.

The rules on continuing to work with children while suspended are complex and anybody who is suspended will need to seek up-to-date advice. Employers should take steps to enquire whether an individual is suspended from any register.

Section 70: Voluntary removal from register

Ofsted must comply with a request from a registered provider to be removed from either register. However, the provider cannot be removed if Ofsted has sent the provider a notice of intention to cancel, or a notice cancelling, registration and the time for making an appeal has not expired (see ss.73 and 74). This prohibition on voluntary removal does not apply to Part B of the OCR, i.e. those who have registered voluntarily.

Section 71: Termination of voluntary registration on expiry of prescribed period

Regulations can specify a period after which a person who is on the voluntary OCR can be removed from the register. There is nothing to stop a person reapplying for registration on the expiry of this period. The DfES consultation paper *Ofsted Childcare Register* (DfES and DWP, 2006c) proposes in para.80 that this period will be one year.

Section 72: Protection of children in an emergency

Ofsted can cancel a person's registration, vary or remove a condition, or impose a new condition, on a person's registration in an emergency.

Ofsted has to present information to a magistrate (Justice of the Peace) that a child 'is suffering or is likely to suffer significant harm'; the registered person does not have to be given notice and the proceedings will be in private by virtue of an amendment found in Schedule 2(1) to the Magistrates' Courts Act 1980. Based on the information provided, the magistrate can make an order in writing, which has immediate effect.

Ofsted must serve the order on the registered person by hand or by post as soon as practicable along with information supporting the application to the magistrate and the provider's appeal rights (see s.74).

'Harm' is defined under in s.31(9) of the Children Act 1989. The *Explanatory Notes* summarises this as 'ill treatment or impairment of physical or mental health or physical, intellectual, emotional, social or behavioural development, including impairment which may be suffered from seeing or hearing another person being ill-treated'. 'Significant harm' is defined in s.31(10) 'by reference to the child's health or development as compared to what could reasonably be expected of another child'.

Registration – procedural safeguards

Sections 73 and 74 set out the procedures and the appeal rights when Ofsted intends to take one of the following actions:

- refuse a registration application
- impose a new condition on a person's registration after the initial registration
- vary or remove a condition of a person's registration
- refuse to vary or remove a registration condition
- cancel registration.

Suspension of registration is dealt with under s.69.

Section 73: Procedure for taking certain steps

Ofsted must give 14 days' notice of the proposed action (see above) to the applicant or the registered person. If the applicant or registered person objects, Ofsted must allow for the objection to be heard either orally or in writing before deciding what to do. If the applicant or registered person accepts Ofsted's proposed action before the end of the 14-day period, then the action can be implemented immediately.

If Ofsted decides to take the action, the applicant or registered person must be notified but the decision does not have effect until the time for appealing under s.74 has expired or, if an appeal is brought, until the appeal is determined. Ofsted can implement the proposed action immediately if the applicant or registered person states that an appeal will not be brought.

Section 74: Appeals

Appeals against a proposed action by Ofsted under s.73 are to the CST set up under the Protection of Children Act 1999. See www.carestandardstribunal.gov.uk for more information. An applicant or a registered person may also appeal to the CST against other decisions made by Ofsted. Full details will be set out in regulations. The CST has to confirm the action of Ofsted or determine that the proposed action shall not have effect. The CST may also impose conditions, or vary or remove conditions of a provider's registration in certain circumstances. The Tribunal also hears appeals under s.72 on protecting children in an emergency.

Section 75: Disqualification from registration

Sections 75 and 76 enable regulations to be made that bring disqualification for childcare providers into alignment with similar provisions for working in schools. Regulations will set out the grounds for disqualification from registration. In so doing, the regulations may use existing lists and criteria. It is likely that the regulations will be modelled on the existing regulations The Day Care and Child Minding (Disqualification) (England) Regulations 2005 (England. Statutory Instruments, 2005b). Disqualified individuals will be those who are included in, or subject, to:

- Protection of Children Act 1999 (POCA) List
- List 99 of individuals unsuitable to work with children
- various orders relating to child protection (there will be a list in the regulations)
- a previous refusal to register or cancellation of registration either under the Childcare Act 2006 or the previous legislation, Parts 10 and 10A of the Children Act 1989
- disqualification from fostering a child either through a local authority or privately

- a decision by a local authority to assume parental rights and responsibility for a child of the applicant

- a conviction for a prescribed offence, or a caution in respect of a prescribed offence (there will be a list in the regulations).

The regulations will list the prescribed offences and other matters in respect of which convictions, orders or determinations have been made that will lead to someone being disqualified from registration.

In addition, a person may be disqualified by living in the same household as someone who is disqualified or if a disqualified person is employed in the household. Full details will be set out in regulations. If a person becomes disqualified through living in the same household as a disqualified person but did not know, and had no reasonable grounds for knowing, that a member of the household was disqualified, then this can be used as a defence against conviction under s.76. The same applies if a disqualified person is employed in the household.

Ofsted will have the power, subject to regulations, to waive a person's disqualification. The person must have first disclosed the grounds for disqualification to Ofsted. See s.102 for extending the scope of disqualification of registration prior to the commencement of s.75.

Section 76: Consequences of disqualification

The consequences of disqualification apply not only to provision where registration is required under ss.33 (early years childminding), 34 (early years provision), 52 (later years childminding) and 53 (later years provision) but also to exempt school-based provision where registration is not required. A disqualified person may not provide such provision or have a role in the management of such provision. Similarly, a person may not employ a disqualified person to help provide childcare. In both cases, an offence is committed. A person (a disqualified person and/or the employer) is liable on summary conviction to a period of imprisonment or a fine not exceeding level 5 on the standard scale (51 weeks' imprisonment or £5000 in November 2006).

See s.75 for the consequences of living in the same household as a disqualified person and the defence against conviction under s.76.

Childcare Act 2006: the essential guide

Note that a person who is disqualified under s.75 cannot be registered on the voluntary OCR by virtue of section 63(3)(a).

Section 77: Powers of entry

Sections 77 to 79 give Ofsted wide powers to enter premises, including domestic premises, to inspect childcare provision including provision which is alleged to be unlicensed.

At a reasonable time, Ofsted has wide powers to enter:

- unregistered premises to check on childcare provision if there is a suspicion that the provision should be registered

- registered premises for the purpose of inspection under ss.49 and 60

- registered premises for the purpose of checking whether conditions of registration have been met.

The latter power can be used to check whether any conditions imposed by s.66 on a person registered on the voluntary part of the OCR are being met. See s.78 for entry where the provision is in domestic premises.

HMCI has to authorise inspectors to do this work. Such inspectors need not be Ofsted employees. Authorised inspectors are given wide powers to inspect premises, take copies of records, seize documents that may be needed as evidence, talk to any children and inspect the arrangements being made for their welfare, and interview the provider and staff. Inspectors must be able to produce a document to show that they have been authorised by HMCI to do this work if required to do so.

If an authorised inspector is obstructed intentionally, then the person doing the obstructing is liable on summary conviction to a fine not exceeding level 4 on the standard scale (£2500 in November 2006).

Section 78: Requirement for consent to entry

The right to enter premises under s.77 to check whether unregistered childcare is being provided is not restricted to the type of premises. However, if registered provision is being provided in a domestic property, for example children who are looked after in their own home or in the home of their childminder, the consent of an adult occupying the property is required prior to entry. Ofsted may impose a registration condition requiring a provider to obtain the necessary consent to entry from the owner of the premises.

Section 79: Power of constable to assist in exercise of powers of entry

An inspector authorised under s.77 to enter premises may apply to the courts for a warrant to enable the police to assist with the inspection. The court (which may be the High Court, county court, or magistrates' court) may issue a warrant if the inspector has attempted to enter the premises but has been prevented from doing so or is likely to be prevented from doing so. The warrant authorises the use of reasonable force by the police, if this is necessary.

Section 80: Combined reports

Sections 80 to 84 provide further legislation on inspection reports and the supply of information.

Ofsted can combine an inspection report of an early years provider with that of any later years provision being made by the same provider. Thus, a single report can be written for a private provider who runs full daycare provision for under fives and an after-school club on the same premises. Section 80 written in order to enable Ofsted to produce a combined report from several inspections, for example where a single body is providing early years provision over a number of sites or to produce an area report. Schedule 2(44) amends s.59 of the Education Act 2005 to enable, for example, a report on early years provision for children aged 2 and under in a maintained school to be combined with a section 5 (of the 2005 Act) school inspection report.

The Education and Inspections Act 2006 s.152 prospectively replaces s.80 with a much wider power for Ofsted to publish combined reports. When the new provision commences, s.59 of the Education Act 2005 will apply to Wales only.

Section 81: Information to be included in annual reports

Ofsted is required to report annually to the Secretary of State on early years and later years provision, and may submit a report at any time. The Education and Inspections Act s.121 will replace s.81 with a much wider duty on Ofsted to report annually to the Secretary of State and a general power to publish reports.

Section 82: Supply of information to Chief Inspector

Ofsted can require information from a registered person (including a person registered on the voluntary OCR) about his/her activities as an early years or later years provider. The information has to be necessary for Ofsted to fulfil its registration and inspection functions.

Section 83: Supply of information to HMRC and local authorities

When a person's application is granted, cancelled (or notice given of intention to cancel), suspended or removed from the register, Ofsted must supply prescribed information from the register to:

- Her Majesty's Revenue and Customs (HMRC) for tax credits to fund childcare provision

- the local authority for the information service established under s.12 (Duty to provide information, advice and assistance).

Regulations will detail the information that may be supplied to HMRC or Ofsted. The regulations are likely to follow the Child Minding and Day Care (Disclosure Functions) (England) Regulations 2004 (2004/3136) (England. Statutory Instruments, 2004).

The information that the DfES proposes to specify in regulations is found in para.30 of the *Childcare Bill: Part 3 – Childcare Regulation and Inspection Arrangements* (DfES, 2006d) as follows:

- the name of the registered person and, if different, the business name under which the childcare is provided or by which the setting is generally known

- the address of the childcare provider and, if different, the address of the premises at which the childcare is provided

- any contact telephone number or email address for the provider (local authorities only)

- any unique reference number used by Ofsted

- the date of the registration, and which of the registers applies

- the date and any reference number attached to the current registration certificate

- the status of the registration, and in particular whether the registration is subject to a cancellation or notice of cancellation, a suspension or a removal from the register on request of the provider

- information on the hours of operation and the age range of the children using the provision – HMRC may not need this information

- any conditions of registration – HMRC will not need this information

- information relating to the quality of the childcare provided, for example the grade given at the last inspection – HMRC will not need this information

- information as to any enforcement action taken against the childcare provider – HMRC will not need this information.

The regulations will make it clear that Ofsted is not required to pass on information relating to the identity of individual children or parents without appropriate consent. Ofsted will not pass on unreliable information.

Section 84: Disclosure of information for certain purposes

Ofsted can supply prescribed information to:

- parents, and bodies working with parents and prospective parents, to help with the choice of childcare

- bodies working to protect children from harm and neglect (set out in regulations).

This is a new function. The information that the DfES proposes to specify in regulations is found in para.33 of the *Childcare Bill: Part 3 – Childcare Regulation and Inspection Arrangements* (DfES, 2006d) as follows:

- information about the childcare setting

- the date and any reference number attached to the current registration certificate

- the status of the registration, and in particular whether the registration is subject to a cancellation or notice of cancellation, a suspension or other enforcement action taken against the provider, or a removal from the register on request of the provider

- any conditions of registration

- information relating to the quality of the childcare provided.

The DfES note states that local authorities, adoption and fostering agencies, and other organisations involved in the regulation of children's services are entitled to receive the information. The regulations will also enable Ofsted to pass on a wider range of information to the police and local authority and other child protection services where there is a need to protect children from harm and neglect. The information could relate to the suitability of a person to look after or be in contact with children.

Offences and criminal proceedings

Sections 85 to 88 provide for an offence of making a misleading statement, set time limits on offences, and clarify who commits an offence when the registered 'person' is not an individual person. Although the Childcare Act refers throughout to a person registering and providing childcare, this is the legal definition of a 'person' and includes a company, corporate charity and an unincorporated association.

Section 85: Offence of making false or misleading statement

It is an offence to make knowingly a false or misleading statement in an application for registration. Persons found guilty of the offence are liable to a fine not exceeding level 5 on the standard scale (£5,000 in November 2006).

Section 86: Time limit for proceedings

A prosecution must be bought within six months of a prosecutor deciding there is sufficient evidence to prosecute, and proceedings must be brought within three years of the alleged offence.

Section 87: Offences by bodies corporate

Although a childminder will be a single named individual and prosecuted as such for any offence under the Act, other persons providing early years provision or later years provision will often be a charity, a company or a group of people operating as an unincorporated association. Section 87 deals with the case where the person is a corporate body, mainly a registered company or a charity with corporate status, and an offence is committed under Part 3 of the Act. This will include a school governing body when providing daycare for children aged two and under. This section applies where the corporate body is found guilty of an offence. If it can be shown that the offence was caused by the consent, connivance or neglect of a person working on behalf of the corporate body (whether or not a member of the body) then that person is also guilty of an offence and is personably liable for the consequences. In such a case both the corporate body and the member of staff who causes the offence to be committed are both liable. Corporate bodies can still be found guilty of an offence even though the offence was committed by an employee. Members of corporate bodies need to take their responsibilities seriously for ensuring that staff are aware of relevant statutory requirements.

Section 88: Unincorporated associations

Much childcare provision will be organised by two or more individuals working together as an unincorporated association and s.88 makes provision for how such childcare providers are to be treated for legal proceedings for offences under Part 3 of the Act. Proceedings must be brought against the organisation as though it were a corporate body, using its name rather than the name of individual members. Similarly, if there is a fine to pay, the unincorporated association is to be treated as if it were a corporate body and the payment of any fine is to come out of the association's funds. As with corporate bodies in s.87, if it can be shown that the offence was caused by the consent, connivance or neglect of a person working on behalf of the association (whether or not a member of the association) then that person is also guilty of an offence and is personally liable for the consequences.

Section 89: Fees

Regulations will prescribe the fees that must be paid to Ofsted for registration on one of the registers, and when the fees must be paid. The regulations will also specify when fees can be waived or varied. The fee structure for the new registration and inspection system will be subject to a wide review before it is introduced in 2008. However, the DfES has given an indication of its plans for the EYR and OCR (DfES, 2006e).

Early Years Register fees

A new fee structure was introduced in October 2006 by way of The Day Care and Child Minding (Registration Fees) (England) (Amendment) Regulations 2006 (SI 2006/2081).

The October 2006 fees (and 2005 fees for comparison) are shown in Table 7 along with the significant Government subsidy of the registration and inspection system.

Table 7 Fee structure from October 2006 compared to 2005

	2005	2006
Daycare provider application fee – more than four hours a day	£121	£150
Daycare provider application fee – less than four hours a day	£14	£18
Childminder application fee	£14	£18
Daycare provider annual fee – more than four hours a day	£94	£120
Daycare provider annual fee – less than four hours a day	£11	£14
Childminder annual fee	£11	£14
Income from fees as a proportion of regulation costs	3.5%	3.9%

Registration fees meet only a small proportion of the cost of registration and inspection and the DfES (2006e, para.3.1) proposed the following strategy for future fee rises:

• a phased move away from a system of large government subsidies to one where providers pay a greater share of the cost of registration

- the introduction of fairer, more flexible and targeted arrangements so that fees better reflect the cost of the service and that subsidies are directed at those who need them

- whether local authorities could assume a higher profile role in subsidy arrangements, determining the extent of subsidy offered based on knowledge of their local providers, in the light of their strengthened responsibility for facilitating the local childcare market.

OCR fees

An indication of the level of fees for the OCR is given in the DfES consultation paper *The Ofsted Childcare Register* (DfES and DWP, 2006c) and the accompanying Regulatory Impact Assessment (DfES, 2006h). Paragraph 27 states that the OCR should operate at full cost recovery and the Regulatory Impact Assessment indicates that the fees will be in the region of £180 per provider each year (para.24), but 'the actual level of fees will be determined as part of the wider review of fees'.

Section 90: Cases where consent to disclosure withheld

Ofsted may need to get information from third parties, such as a previous employer, before making a decision on whether to register a provider or cancel a provider's registration. Often the information will be confidential and the applicant's or provider's consent is required before the third party can disclose information to Ofsted. Section 90 states that if the applicant or provider refuses to give consent to the disclosure of information, then in circumstances to be determined by regulations, Ofsted can refuse or cancel registration. See 'Prescribed requirements for registration' on page 68.

The DfES intends, after consultation, that the regulations will replace the existing list of possible third-party checks found in the Day Care and Child Minding (Suitability) (England) Regulations 2005 (England. Statutory Instruments, 2005d). The list can be found in Annex A of the DfES note: *Childcare Bill: Part 3 – Childcare Regulation and Inspection Arrangements* (DfES, 2006d).

Section 91: Cooperation between authorities

This section gives Ofsted the power to request a local authority to take a specified action to help Ofsted. The local authority must comply with the request if the action is compatible with the local authority's statutory and other duties and does not unduly affect the discharge of any functions. Local authorities have wide powers to cooperate with other LAs under local government legislation and this is not changed by this section.

This section replaces the provision found at Schedule 9A(8) of the Children Act 1989 and is rarely used. It provides a fallback should an LA not help Ofsted with the registration and supervision of childcare providers. Clearly, the LA's local knowledge is invaluable to Ofsted when pursuing childminders for non-registration. A local authority can decline a request on the grounds that the request might breach the authority's duties under the Data Protection Act or that the request might lead to significant extra work and stops the local authority performing, for example, other duties such as those under s.12 (Duty to provide information, advice and assistance).

Section 92: Combined certificates of registration

Ofsted can combine registration certificates (see ss. 37, 56 and 64). Thus a person who provides full-time childcare for under fives with an after-school club for older children will have a single registration certificate, rather than two or three certificates.

Section 93: Notices

This section mainly applies to notices under s.73 (Procedure for taking certain steps), namely notices given by Ofsted to refuse registration, impose or vary conditions or cancel registration, or a notice to Ofsted that an applicant does not intend to appeal. It also applies to voluntary removal from the register (s.70), and applications to be included on another part of the register (s.65) or another part of the OCR (ss.57 and 65). Section 93 does not apply to enforcement notices issued under ss.33 and 52, i.e. notices requiring a provider to register.

Notices may be hand delivered, sent by post or emailed. Ofsted can only use email if the applicant or registered person has agreed to use email and has provided an address. Emails to Ofsted must be in accordance with Ofsted's requirements.

Section 94: Power to amend Part 3 – applications in respect of multiple premises

The Secretary of State can use the affirmative resolution procedure (see s.105) to amend Part 3 of the Act to allow a single registration to include more than one set of premises, for example, a company providing early years provision on several sites may be able to have a single registration rather than register each site separately. Until the law is changed, the company will have to register each site separately (and not in the name of the employee who is in charge of each site but in the name of the company). This will not apply to childminders.

Section 95: Certain institutions not to be regarded as schools

Where an early years provider provides only early years provision then the provision is not to be regarded as a school (within the terms of the statutory definition of a school found in s.4 of the Education Act 1996). This does not apply to an LA-maintained nursery school or the 'school' status of a school that provides early years provision. What it does mean is that an independent early years provider is not a school (within the terms of the statutory definition of a school), although there is nothing to stop the 'Little Squirrels School' continuing to use the name.

Section 96: Meaning of early years and later years provision, etc.

Section 96 contains important definitions used in Part 3 of the Act.

Early years provision is childcare for a young child, that is childcare for a child up to the day before the 1 September after his or her 5th birthday. Given that the policy of some schools and local authorities is to admit children into reception classes soon after a child's 4th birthday, it is possible for a child to spend nearly two years in reception and year 1 while still coming within the definition of early years provision.

Early years and later years childminding is defined as provision on domestic premises for reward as long as the number of persons providing childcare does not exceed three, i.e. the childminder and no more than two other people. If the number of persons exceeds three then the provision has to be registered as 'other' provision.

The upper age limit for later years provision is also defined in s.96. See also 'Upper age limit of later years provision' in the introduction to Part 3, chapter 4 (page 88).

Section 97: Employees not regarded as providing childcare

An employee of a company, charity, unincorporated partnership, etc cannot be the registered provider for early years or later years childcare provision. The employer must be the registered provider. This clarifies that it is the employer who has responsibility for ensuring that:

- the EYFS is provided for early years provision and the welfare requirements are met for later years provision

- employees are not disqualified from registration.

Employing someone who is disqualified is an offence under s.76 (Consequences of disqualification) and under ss.87 or 88 the employer is corporately responsible.

Section 98: Interpretation

Section 98 mainly provides references to where statutory terms are described in this and other Acts. Mention has already been made (see page 60) of the definition of the 'Chief Inspector'.

Two terms are reused from the Children Act 1989:

- 'domestic premises', which means premises that are used wholly or mainly as a private dwelling

- 'premises', which includes any area and any vehicle.

The latter is helpful as it means a vehicle can be the address for childcare provision, for example a mobile crèche.

Part 4

Miscellaneous and general

Miscellaneous and general information

Part 4 contains important legislation on enabling data to be collected and used mainly for planning purposes (ss.99 to 101). Section 102 extends the disqualification arrangements for childcare workers. The remaining sections cover standard items in all legislation.

Provision of information about children

Sections 99 and 100 provide for the Secretary of State to make regulations to collect information about young children (see s.19) in England participating in the 'free entitlement' to nursery education under s.118 of School Standards and Framework Act 1998. This will become the 'free entitlement' to childcare (see page 31) once s.7 of the Childcare Act 2006 commences in September 2008). Section 101 achieves the same for Wales although in Wales the terminology will not change.

The Government want the information collected to help with

• the allocation of funding to LAs

• local and national planning of childcare provision

• supporting LAs in England in meeting their new duties to improve well-being and reduce inequalities between young children.

For reasons of accuracy and consistency, the Government wants data collected on an individual child basis, i.e. a data record for each child is to be transmitted electronically to the DfES via the LA. The Schools Census (formerly known as the PLASC – the Pupil Level Annual Schools Census) has achieved this for young children attending maintained schools since 2002. The legislative authority is in s.537A of the Education Act 1996; this will be replaced by s.99 in 2008. The two sections are similar in respect of who can collect data, and to whom the data can be sent and the purposes for which a body may use the data.

Information on young children attending private, voluntary and independent sector provision is collected through the Early Years Census but only at an aggregate level, i.e. information on individual children is put together before it is submitted. The combined effect of ss. 99 to 101 is to allow information to be returned at pupil level for the private, voluntary and independent sectors. The purpose of s.100 is to enable this to happen before the new LA duties (and the terminology) commence in 2008.

The DfES has consulted on draft regulations (see www.dfes.gov.uk/consultations/conDetails.cfm?consultationId=1412). The intention is that the regulations will commence in 2007 to enable a pilot to be done prior to data being collected from all LAs in January 2008. Regulations under s.99 (but not s.101 for Wales) can be used for collecting data on all children attending early years provision. There will be further consultation before this commences.

With regard to supporting LAs in England in meeting their new duties to improve well-being and reduce inequalities of young children, information is already collected on the Foundation Stage profile (FSP) scores for each child in July following the child's fifth birthday. Local authorities submit aggregated LA level data together with a 10 per cent randomised sample of full results to the DfES. This is not yet part of the Schools Census. The consultation on the draft regulations states that the DfES intends to collect the full FSP results in due course.

Section 99: Provision of information about young children – England

The Secretary of State can make regulations to require all registered early years providers including school-based providers who are exempt from registration requirements under s.34(2) to provide individual child information to the Secretary of State or any prescribed person. The draft regulations indicate that the LA will be a prescribed person.

Section 99 also provides for individual child information to be shared between the Secretary of State, an information collator (an organisation collating data on behalf of the Government), any other persons prescribed by the regulations, or people in any categories prescribed by the regulations. The draft regulations indicate the following will be prescribed: Ofsted, the QCA (and National Assessment Agency), the relevant LA and the relevant school.

Section 99(7) provides one safeguard in that information received under the section cannot be published in any form that includes the name of the child or children to whom the information relates. The provisions of the Data Protection Act also apply.

During debates in Parliament, the Minister (Lord Adonis) gave further information about how this section would work in practice, in response to arguments that too much of the detail was left to secondary legislation:

We will carry out a full consultation and impact assessment on how the information-collection provisions will work in practice and what information we will want to collect from providers. However, it is likely to include similar information to that already collected though the PLASC [Pupil Level Annual School Census] such as child's name, date of birth, address, gender and ethnicity, and hours of attendance, type of setting and Foundation Stage profile data, which are currently collected at an aggregate level through other surveys. The provisions will simplify and improve current data-collection processes, reducing burdens on local authorities.
Hansard. HL, 2006l, c.82

The Minister added that the Government sees no gain in bringing these data-collection proposals together with the information-sharing index being established under s.12 of the Children Act 2004. The information-sharing index under s.12 is a tool to help practitioners (including registered childcare providers) work together to meet the needs of individual children. Information is collected under the Childcare Act provisions for strategic purposes.

Section 100: Provision of information about young children – transitory provisions

Section 100 amends s.99 for the period up to the start of the new arrangements in September 2008. During the interim period, data may be collected only on children receiving funded nursery education under s.118 of the School Standards and Framework Act 1998. Data about 3 and 4 year olds in maintained schools will be collected under regulations made under s.537A of the Education Act 1996.

Section 101: Provision of information about children – Wales

Section 101 applies to Wales and allows for regulations to be made to require all childminders and daycare providers registered under Part 10A of the Children Act 1989, and providers of funded nursery education, to provide individual child information to the Assembly or any prescribed person. Section 101 also provides for individual child information to be shared by the Assembly, an information collator (an organisation collating data on behalf of the Assembly), any other persons prescribed by the regulations, or people in any categories prescribed by the regulations. Section 101(7) provides the safeguard that information received by or under s.101, cannot be published in any form that includes the name of the child or children to whom the information relates. The provisions of the Data Protection Act also apply.

Consultation on the collection of data from providers of funded nursery education will not take place before the consultation on the Foundation Phase in Wales in early 2007. The first data collection in Wales is likely to take place in 2008. No timetable has been agreed for registered childcare providers who are not funded for nursery education.

Section 102: Disqualification for registration under Children Act 1989

Section 102 amends Schedule 9A of the Children Act 1989 in order to disqualify people from registering as daycare providers or childminders who previously were outside the scope of the regulation-making power in Schedule 9A. Once this section has commenced, regulations will be able to disqualify individuals:

- on health grounds (who are already disqualified from work in schools by a direction under s.142 of the Education Act 2002, commonly known as List 99 and which leads to disqualification from working with other children's services through inclusion on the Protection of Children Act list)

- who have been given a caution (including a reprimand or warning within the meaning of s.65 of the Crime and Disorder Act 1998) for a prescribed offence, which will be listed in the regulations.

As changes are being made to List 99 (by including new offences that will merit automatic disqualification), additional individuals will be barred from working in daycare settings and as childminders. However, the barring will not be made retrospectively, but Ofsted will disqualify individuals as unsuitable to work with children if they have been convicted of a relevant offence or received a caution prior to the implementation. Consequential changes will be made to the regulations to reduce the offences and cautions where Ofsted can waive the disqualification.

These changes will have a short-term application for England prior to the full implementation of the new childcare registers from September 2008 when s.75 will apply. In Wales, disqualification from daycare and childminding will continue to rely on schedule 9A of the Children Act 1989.

Section 103 and Schedule 2 and 3: Minor and consequential amendments and repeals

Schedule 2 contains 'minor and consequential' amendments to other legislation and Schedule 3 lists repeals of other legislation.

A large number of the amendments, principally to the Children Act 1989 and the School Standards and Framework Act 1998, repeal or amend the current legislation so that it only applies to Wales. For example, para.30 makes s.118 of the School Standards and Framework Act 1998, on an LA ensuring sufficient nursery education provision, apply only to Wales.

Another group of amendments changes the statutory term 'relevant nursery education' to 'relevant early years education', thus making it clear that the benefits that were available to young children in the 'free entitlement' to nursery education will continue (in October 2006 12.5 hours a week for 38 weeks a years for 3- and 4-year-olds). This covers assessment of special educational needs (para.24), LA travel arrangements (para.23), school meals (para.24) and protection from corporal punishment (para.27).

To the reader, paragraphs 25 and 26 are exactly the same except that they amend two different sections of the Education Act 1996, although confusingly both sections have the same title. The paragraphs cover the powers of the LA and school governing body to provide qualified teachers and equipment used for teaching to 'day nurseries' provided by the LA under s.18 of the Children Act 1989. Paragraph 4 amends s.18 of the 1989 Act to prevent a local authority in England providing daycare for children under 5 and not attending school except when the children are in need. Similarly, for children of compulsory school age, the LA can only provide appropriate care and supervised activities when the children are in need. Clearly, this is in response to the Government's drive to create a market in childcare provision for the under fives, although the amendments appear to support the 'poor law' origins of the legislation that public provision should only be for children in need.

Childcare Act 2006: the essential guide

The Serious Organised Crime and Police Act 2005 rewrote and consolidated the provisions of the Police Act 1997, which established the current regime of criminal record checking. The Police Act is further amended to allow criminal record checks to be part of Ofsted's and employers' decisions on suitability of individuals to work with children under the age of 8.

The amendment to the School Standards and Framework Act 1998 at para.35 makes clear that early years provision will continue into the reception class and 'any more senior class'. One consequence of this is the amendment (found at para.42) to s.176 of the Education Act 2002, which provides for consultation with pupils. The effect is to raise the age at which pupils will be required to be consulted as all pupils in early years education will be excluded from consultation. However, s.176 has been further amended by the Education and Inspections Act 2006, s.167, to require consultation with all under fives in maintained schools.

A person on the early years or Ofsted childcare registers will be able to make disclosures to the information databases established under s.12 of the Children Act 2004, commonly known as Information Sharing and Assessment (ISA).

Finally, premises used for the provision of childcare (but not childminding) cannot have their water cut off for non-payment of charges. Paragraph 19 makes this amendment to the Water Industry Act 1991.

Section 104: Subordinate legislation – general provision

The Act refers to additional or secondary legislation in the form of regulations or orders that the Secretary of State or the National Assembly for Wales can make (although this will change when the Government of Wales Act 2006 is implemented) by statutory instrument (see s.105). Often, this is referred to in the Act as a power given to the Secretary of State to prescribe information or rules. See s.98 for the definition of 'prescribed', i.e. prescribed by regulations. An example is s.35(2)(a), which provides for 'prescribed' information to be supplied by applicants for the Early Years Registers. The information will be found in regulations to be made by the Secretary of State.

Section 104(2) contains the usual rules on the order or regulation-making powers:

• different provisions may be made for different cases or areas

- provision can be both generally or in relation to specific cases

- transitional provisions from the current regulations, etc can be made.

Section 105: Subordinate legislation – parliamentary control

A statutory instrument is the formal document made by the Secretary of State or Assembly setting out the secondary legislation. In England, the statutory instrument has to be laid before Parliament and if either the Commons or the Lords passes a resolution annulling the instrument, then the secondary legislation falls. This is the negative resolution procedure and it is a very rare event for a statutory instrument to be annulled. The resolution should be passed within 40 parliamentary days of the Instrument being made.

Commencement orders under s.109 are not subject to this type of direct parliamentary scrutiny.

Three order-making powers are subject to greater parliamentary scrutiny called the affirmative resolution procedure, that is both Houses of Parliament have to pass a resolution affirming the order before it can take effect. The powers are in:

- s.5 – to amend the definition of early childhood services

- s.41 – to amend the areas of learning and development in the Early Years Foundation Stage

- s.94 – to allow for the registration of multiple premises by a single provider.

Section 106: General interpretation

Contains standard definitions used in the Act by reference to a section in the Act or earlier legislation. Two definitions are worthy of comment. The definition of 'child' means a person under the age of 18, that is unless otherwise specified, which it usually is, the Act provides for children up until their 18th birthday. See page 93 for 'Upper age limit of later years provision'.

The one self-contained definition in the Act is that of the 'English local authority'. However, this is the same definition as is used for:

- 'children's services authority in England' (found in s.65 of the Children Act 2004)

- 'local education authority' (as applied to England) in s.12 of the Education Act 1996 (and s.581 for the Isles of Scilly).

Section 107: Financial provisions

A standard provision to fund the Act's implementation.

Sections 108: Isles of Scilly

The Secretary of State can by order except, adapt or modify provisions within Part 1 and Part 3 in their application to the Isles of Scilly.

Sections 109: Commencement

Before each section of the Act can come into force it must be 'commenced'. Section 109 commenced ss.104 to 111 on Royal Assent (11 July 2006). The dates on which the other sections can come into force will be made in accordance with an order under s.110 (which in England has no direct parliamentary scrutiny – see s.105).

Section 110: The appropriate authority by whom commencement order is made

This defines which provisions in the Act are the responsibility of the Secretary of State to commence for England and which provisions are the responsibility of the National Assembly for Wales to commence for Wales.

Section 111: Short title and extent

The short title of the Act is the Childcare Act 2006 and it extends to England and Wales only, as does the extent of any amendment by the Act to other legislation.

References

Bryson, S. (2005). *Walking with Children*. Newcastle: Armstrong Sure Start Local Programme.

Department for Education and Skills (2002). *Birth to Three Matters: an Introduction to the Framework* [online]. Available: http://www.standards.dfes.gov.uk/primary/publications/foundation_stage/940463/ss_birth2_3matters_birth.pdf [6 November, 2006].

Department for Education and Skills (2005a). *Childcare Bill Consultation. Consultation on Legislative Proposals for the Future of Childcare and Early Years Provision in England: Implementing the Ten Year Strategy* [online]. Available: http://www.dfes.gov.uk/consultations/downloadableDocs/Childcare%20Bill%20Consultation.pdf [6 November, 2006].

Department for Education and Skills (2005b). *Sure Start Children's Centre Practice Guidance* [online]. Available: www.surestart.gov.uk/publications/?Document=1500)[6 November, 2006].

Department for Education and Skills (2006a). *Consultation on Draft Regulations Setting Out the Process for Setting Statutory Targets for Local Authorities Under the Childcare Act 2006* [online]. Available: http://www.dfes.gov.uk/consultations/conDetails.cfm?consultationId=1419 [6 November, 2006].

Department for Education and Skills (2006b). *Childcare Bill: Duty to Improve Well-Being and Reduce Inequalities in Outcomes for Children up to 5* (Statutory Guidance - Draft Outline) [online]. Available: http://www.surestart.gov.uk/_doc/P0002086.pdf [6 November, 2006]. cited on page 26, 32

Department for Education and Skills (2006c). *Childcare Bill: Duty to Secure Sufficient Childcare* [online]. Available: http://www.surestart.gov.uk/_doc/P0002083.pdf [6 November, 2006].

Department for Education and Skills (2006d). *Childcare Bill: Part 3 – Childcare Regulation and Inspection Arrangements* [online]. Available: http://www.surestart.gov.uk/_doc/P0002175.pdf [6 November, 2006].

Department for Education and Skills (2006e). *Childcare Registration: Fees Proposal* [online]. Available: http://www.dfes.gov.uk/consultations/conResults.cfm?consultationId=1383 [6 November, 2006].

Department for Education and Skills (2006f). *A Code of Practice on the Provision of Free Nursery Education Places for Three- and Four-Year-Olds* [online]. Available: http:www.surestart.gov.uk/_doc/P0002205.pdf [6 November, 2006].

Department for Education and Skills (2006g). *Exemptions Power* [Relating to the Childcare Act 2006] [online]. Available: http://www.surestart.gov.uk/_doc/P0001899.pdf [6 November, 2006].

Department for Education and Skills (2006h). *Final Regulatory Impact Assessment for the Childcare Act 2006* [online]. Available: http://www.dfes.gov.uk/ria/assessmentFiles/riaFile_74.pdf [6 November, 2006].

Department for Education and Skills (2006i). *Joint Commissioning Framework and Guidance on the Children and Young People's Plan* [online]. Available: http://www.changeforchildren.co.uk/uploads/DfES_Commissioning_Briefing_Paper.doc [7 November, 2006].

Department for Education and Skills (2006j). *Planning and Funding Extended Schools: a Guide for Local Authorities and their Partner Organisations* [online]. Available: http://publications.teachernet.gov.uk/eOrderingDownload/DFES-0472-2006.pdf [6 November, 2006].

Department for Education and Skills (2006k). *Provision for Children under Five Years of Age in England: January 2006 (Final)* (Statistical First Release 32/2006) [online]. Available: http://www.dfes.gov.uk/rsgateway/DB/SFR/s000674/index.shtml [6 November, 2006].

Department for Education and Skills (2006l) *Schools and Pupils in England: January 2006 (Final)* (Statistical First Release 38/2006) [online]. Available: http://www.dfes.gov.uk/rsgateway/DB/SFR/s000682/SFR38-2006.pdf [6 November, 2006].

Department For Education and Skills and Department for Work and Pensions (2003). *Childminding. National Standards for Under 8s Day Care and Childminding* [online]. Available: http://www.childcarelink.gov.uk/pdf/ofsted/Module2.pdf [6 November, 2006].

Department for Education and Skills and Department for Work and Pensions (2006a). *Choice for Parents, the Best Start for Children: Making it Happen. An Action Plan for the Ten Year Strategy: Sure Start Children's Centres, Extended Schools and Childcare* [online]. Available: http://www.everychildmatters.gov.uk/_files/06EA29398072BE73E834DBA061584307.pdf [6 November, 2006].

Department for Education and Skills and Department for Work and Pensions (2006b). *The Early Years Foundation Stage: Consultation on a Single Quality Framework for Services to Children from Birth to Five* [online]. Available: http://www.dfes.gov.uk/consultations/conResults.cfm?consultationId=1393 [6 November, 2006].

Department for Education and Skills and Department for Work and Pensions (2006c). *The Ofsted Childcare Register – a Consultation Paper* [online]. Available: http://www.dfes.gov.uk/consultations/conResults.cfm?consultationId=1410 [6 November, 2006].

England. Statutory Instruments (2001). *Child Minding and Day Care (Certificate of Registration) (England) Regulations 2001* (SI 2001/1830). London: The Stationery Office.

England. Statutory Instruments (2003a). *The Child Minding and Day Care (Suspension of Registration) (England) Regulations 2003* (SI 2003/332). London: The Stationery Office.

England. Statutory Instruments (2003b). *The Day Care and Child Minding (National Standards) (England) Regulations 2003*(SI 2003/1996). London: The Stationery Office.

England. Statutory Instruments (2003c). *Education (Nursery Education and Early Years Development) (England) (Amendment) Regulations 2003* (SI 2003/2939) [online]. Available: http://www.opsi.gov.uk/SI/si2003/20032939.htm [6 November, 2006].

England. Statutory Instruments (2004). *The Child Minding and Day Care (Disclosure Functions) (England) Regulations 2004*. London: The Stationery Office.

England. Statutory Instruments (2005a). *The Day Care and Child Minding (Inspection) (England) Regulations 2005* (SI 2005/2300). London: The Stationery Office.

England. Statutory Instruments (2005b). *The Day Care and Child Minding (Disqualification) (England) Regulations 2005* (SI 2005/2296). London: The Stationery Office.

England. Statutory Instruments (2005c). *The Day Care and Child Minding (National Standards) (Amendment) (England) Regulations 2005* (SI 2005/2303). London: The Stationery Office.

England. Statutory Instruments (2005d). *The Day Care and Child Minding (Suitability) (England) Regulations 2005* (SI 2005/2297). London: The Stationery Office.

England. Statutory Instruments (2005e). *The Nursery Education (Inspection) (England) Regulations 2005* (SI 2005/2299). London: The Stationery Office.

Gershon, P. (2004). *Releasing Resources to the Frontline: Independent Review of Public Sector Efficiency* [online]. Available: www.hm-treasury.gov.uk./media/B2C/11/efficiency_review120704.pdf [6 November, 2006].

Great Britain. Parliament. House of Commons (2005). *Higher Standards, Better Schools for All: More Choice for Parents and Pupils* (Cm. 6677). London: The Stationery Office.

Hampton, P. (2005). *Reducing Administrative Burdens: Effective Inspection and Enforcement* (The Hampton Review) [online]. Available: http://www.hm-treasury.gov.uk./media/A63/EF/bud05hamptonv1.pdf [6 November, 2006].

Hansard. House of Commons (2005a). 'Childcare Bill', *House of Commons Standing Committee D*, 8 December 2005, Clause 6 c120 Deb [online]. Available: http://www.publications.parliament.uk/pa/cm200506/cmstand/d/st051208/pm/512 08s02.htm#end [7 November, 2006].

Hansard. House of Commons (2005b). 'Childcare Bill', *House of Commons Standing Committee D*, 8 December 2005, Clause 6 c128 Deb [online]. Available: http://www.publications.parliament.uk/pa/cm200506/cmstand/d/st051208/pm/512 08s03.htm [7 November, 2006].

Hansard. House of Commons (2005c). 'Childcare Bill', *House of Commons Standing Committee D*, 13 December 2005, Clause 17 c217 Deb [online]. Available: http://www.publications.parliament.uk/pa/cm200506/cmstand/d/st051213/pm/512 13s03.htm [7 November, 2006].

Hansard. House of Commons (2005d). 'Childcare Bill', *House of Commons Standing Committee D*, 15 December 2005, Clause 41 c251 Deb [online]. Available: http://www.publications.parliament.uk/pa/cm200506/cmstand/d/st051215/am/5121 5s02.htm [7 November, 2006].

Hansard. House of Commons (2005e). 'Childcare Bill', *House of Commons Standing Committee D*, 20 December 2005, Clause 79 c307 Deb [online]. Available: http://www.publications.parliament.uk/pa/cm200506/cmstand/d/st051220/am/5122 0s02.htm [7 November, 2006].

Hansard. House of Commons (2006a). 'Childcare Bill', *House of Commons Daily Hansard*, **443**, 121, 9 March 2006, c1033 Deb [online]. Available: http://www.publications.parliament.uk/pa/cm200506/cmhansrd/cm060309/debtext/60309-31.htm# 60309-31_spnew2 [7 November, 2006].

Hansard. House of Commons (2006b). 'Education and Inspections Bill', *House of Commons Standing Committee E*, 11 May 2006, Clause 103 cc911–912 Deb [online]. Available: http://www.publications.parliament.uk/pa/cm200506/cmstand/ e/st060511/pm/60511s03.htm [7 November, 2006].

Hansard. House of Lords (2006a). 'Childcare Bill, committee', *House of Lords Weekly Hansard*, **681**, 136, 26 April 2006, c105 Deb [online]. Available: http://www.publications.parliament.uk/pa/ld200405/ldhansrd/pdvn/lds06/text/6042 6-32.htm [7 November, 2006].

Hansard. House of Lords (2006b). 'Childcare Bill, committee', *House of Lords Weekly Hansard*, **681**, 136, 26 April 2006, c116 Deb [online]. Available: http://www.publications.parliament.uk/pa/ld200405/ldhansrd/pdvn/lds06/text/60426-35.htm#column_GC115 [7 November, 2006].

Hansard. House of Lords (2006c). 'Childcare Bill, committee', *House of Lords Weekly Hansard*, **681**, 136, 26 April 2006, c118 Deb [online]. Available: http://www.publications.parliament.uk/pa/ld200405/ldhansrd/pdvn/lds06/text/60426-35.htm#column_GC115 [7 November, 2006]. Page 32

Hansard. House of Lords (2006d). 'Childcare Bill, committee', *House of Lords Weekly Hansard*, **681**, 140, 4 May 2006, cc286-289 Deb [online]. Available: http://www.publications.parliament.uk/pa/ld200405/ldhansrd/pdvn/lds06/text/60504-27.htm [7 November, 2006].

Hansard. House of Lords (2006e). 'Childcare Bill, committee', *House of Lords Weekly Hansard*, **681**, 140, 4 May 2006, c338 Deb [online]. Available: http://www.publications.parliament.uk/pa/ld200405/ldhansrd/pdvn/lds06/text/60504-41.htm [7 November, 2006].

Hansard. House of Lords (2006f). 'Childcare Bill, committee', *House of Lords Weekly Hansard*, **681**, 140, 4 May 2006, c340 Deb [online]. Available: http://www.publications.parliament.uk/pa/ld200405/ldhansrd/pdvn/lds06/text/60504-41.htm [7 November, 2006].

Hansard. House of Lords (2006g). 'Childcare Bill, committee', *House of Lords Weekly Hansard*, **681**, 140, 4 May 2006, c342 Deb [online]. Available: http://www.publications.parliament.uk/pa/ld200405/ldhansrd/pdvn/lds06/text/60504-42.htm [7 November, 2006].

Hansard. House of Lords (2006h). 'Childcare Bill, committee', *House of Lords Weekly Hansard*, **681**, 140, 4 May 2006, c343 Deb [online]. Available: http://www.publications.parliament.uk/pa/ld200405/ldhansrd/pdvn/lds06/text/60504-42.htm [7 November, 2006].

Hansard. House of Lords (2006i). 'Childcare Bill (report stage)', *House of Lords Weekly Hansard*, **683**, 159, 12 June 2006, c18 Deb [online]. Available: http://www.publications.parliament.uk/pa/ld199697/ldhansrd/pdvn/lds06/text/60612-05.htm [7 November, 2006].

Hansard. House of Lords (2006j). 'Childcare Bill (report stage)'. *House of Lords Weekly Hansard*, **683,** 139, 12 June 2006, c39 Deb [online]. Available: http://www.publications.parliament.uk/pa/ld199697/ldhansrd/pdvn/lds06/text/60612-10.htm [7 November, 2006].

Hansard. House of Lords (2006k). 'Childcare Bill (report stage)', *House of Lords Weekly Hansard*, **683**, 159, 12 June 2006, c18 Deb [online]. Available: http://www.publications.parliament.uk/pa/ld199697/ldhansrd/pdvn/lds06/text/6061 2-05.htm [7 November, 2006].

Hansard. House of Lords (2006l). 'Childcare Bill (report stage)', *House of Lords Weekly Hansard*, **683**, 159, 12 June 2006, c82 Deb [online]. Available: http://www.publications.parliament.uk/pa/ld199697/ldhansrd/pdvn/lds06/text/6061 2-20.htm [7 November, 2006].

Hansard. House of Lords (2006m). 'Childcare Bill (report stage)'. *House of Lords Weekly Hansard*, **683,** 168, 26 June 2006, c1011 W [online]. Available: http://www.publications.parliament.uk/pa/ld200405/ldhansrd/pdvn/lds06/text/6062 6-04.htm#60626-04_head4 [7 November, 2006].

HM Government (2006). *Planning and Funding Extending Schools: a Guide for Schools, Local Authorities and their Partner Organisations*. London: DfES.

HM Treasury (2004). *2004 Spending Review: Public Service Agreements 2005-2008. Chapter 2: Department for Education and Skills* [online]. Available: http://www.hm-treasury.gov.uk/media/12D/57/sr04_psa_ch2.pdf [7 November, 2006].

HM Treasury, Department for Education and Skills, Department for Work and Pensions and Department of Trade and Industry (2004). *Choice for Parents, the Best Start for Children: a Ten Year Strategy for Childcare* [online]. Available: www.hm-treasury.gov.uk./pre_budget_report/prebud_pbr04/assoc_docs/prebud_pbr04_adchi ldcare.cfm [3 November, 2006].

Office for Standards in Education (2006). *Early Years: Safe and Sound* (HMI 2663) [online]. Available: http://live.ofsted.gov.uk/safeandsound/08_documents/safeand-sound.pdf [6 November, 2006].

Qualifications and Curriculum Authority and Department for Education and Employment (2000). *Curriculum Guidance for the Foundation Stage.* London: QCA.

Rose, J. (2006). *Independent Review of the Teaching of Early Reading: Final Report* (Rose Report). London: DfES.

Welsh Assembly Government. Department for Training and Education (2005). The *Childcare Strategy for Wales: Childcare is for Children* (DfTE Information Document No 047-05) [online]. Available: http://www.learning.wales.gov.uk/pdfs/ childcare-strategy-e.pdf [6 November, 2006].

Further reading

Clark, C. (2004). *Why and How we Listen to Young Children* (Listening as a Way of Life Series) [online]. Available: http://www.ncb.org.uk/dotpdf/open%20access%20-%20phase%201%20only/listening-intro_ncb_20050401.pdf [6 November, 2006].

Dickens, M (2004). *Listening to Young Disabled Children* (Listening as a Way of Life Series). London: NCB.

Lancaster, Y. P. (2006). RAMPS: a Framework for Listening to Children. London: Daycare Trust.

McAuliffe, A-M. with Lane, J. (2005). *Listening and Responding to Young Children's Views on Food* (Listening as a Way of Life Series) [online]. Available: http://www.thechildrenshouse.org.uk/pdf/01.pdf [6 November, 2006].

McLarnon, J. (2004). *Supporting Parents and Carers to Listen: a Guide for Practitioners* (Listening as a Way of Life Series) [online]. Available: http://www.ncb.org.uk/dotpdf/open%20access%20-%20phase%201%20only/listening-parents_ncb_20050401.pdf NCB [6 November, 2006].

Rich, D. (2004). *Listening to Babies* (Listening as a Way of Life Series). London: NCB.

Road, N. (2004). *Are Equalities an Issue? Finding Out what Young Children Think* (Listening as a Way of Life Series) [online]. Available: http://www.ncb.org.uk/dotpdf/open%20access%20-%20phase%201%20only/listening-equalities_ncb_20050401.pdf [6 November, 2006].

Glossary

CLL	communication, language and literacy
CRB	Criminal Records Bureau
CSA	Children's Services Authorities
CST	Care Standards Tribunal
CWDC	Children's Workforce Development Council
CWS	Children's Workforce Strategy
DCS	Director of Children's Services
ECM	Every Child Matters
EYR	Early Years Register
EYFS	Early Years Foundation Stage
JAR	Joint Area Review
LA	local authority
OCR	Ofsted Childcare Register
PSED	personal social and emotional development

Index

Entries in *italics* denote publications/initiatives.

2007 start date 5, 7
2008 start date 5, 7, 14, 35
activities 90–1, 95–6
advice 13, 38–40, 51
affordability 3, 28–9
appeals 101
appropriate authorities 123
assessments 35–8, 51, 77–97
assistance 13, 38–40, 51
availability 2

babysitters 65
black communities 7, 30
brokerage service 39

cancellation of registration 97
Care Standards Tribunal (CST) 98, 101
certificates, registration 71–2, 89, 95, 111
charges 29, 34–5, 42, 51
Chief Inspector (Ofsted) 60–3, 105
Chief Inspector (Wales) 52
child, definition 43, 122
childcare, definitions 43–4, 49, 52
childcare provision
    assessments 35–8, 51
    England 25–38
    local authority powers 32–3
    providers 51, 93
    sufficient and affordable 13, 28–9, 50
    sustainable 31
    Wales 49–51
    see also early years provision
Childcare Strategy for Wales 49
childminders 9, 64, 66, 70–1, 87–8, 93, 94
childminding, definition 64
children
    0–5 years 7–8
    5–14 years 5, 8, 56, 93, 94
    information about 116–18
Children Act 1989 119–20
Children Act 2004 41
Children's Centres 9, 12, 17, 21
Children's Information Service (CIS) 8, 38–40

Children's Workforce Development Council (CWDC) 4
Children's Workforce Strategy 2, 4
Children and Young People's Plans (CYPPs) 8, 35–6
CIS *see* Children's Information Service
combined certificates of registration 111

combined reports 104
commencement dates 14, 16, 28, 35, 123
compulsory OCR registration 87–91
    early years providers 89
    exemptions 92–3
    start date 5, 7
consent to entry 103–4
convictions 102
corporate bodies 59, 108
CRB *see* Criminal Records Bureau
crèches 9
criminal proceedings 107–9
Criminal Records Bureau (CRB) 69
CST *see* Care Standards Tribunal
curriculum amendments 82–3
Curriculum Guidance for the Foundation Stage 75
CWDC *see* Children's Workforce Development Council
CYPPs *see* Children and Young People's Plans

development *see* learning and development
disabled children 7, 29, 38, 39, 50, 93
disclosure of information 106–7, 110
disqualification from registration 101–3, 119–20

early childhood services 18–24
early learning goals 76
Early Years Census 116
Early Years Foundation Stage (EYFS) 73–9
    assessment arrangements 77–9
    curriculum amendments 82–3
    duty to implement 74–5
    exemptions 81–2
    learning and development 75–8
    orders 81
    start date 7, 9
early years provision
    charges 29, 42
    definition 44, 112–13
    free of charge 28, 31–2, 33–4, 42, 116
    inspections 83–4
    providers 9, 70–1, 73, 89
    regulation 61, 64–86
    workforce development 4–5
Early Years Register (EYR) 5, 7, 9, 62–3, 64, 70–1, 109–10
ECM *see* *Every Child Matters*
education 43, 76–7
    see also schools
Education and Inspection (E&I) Act 2006 60, 62
emergency protection of children 99–100
employees' status 113

England 12–46, 117–18
entitlement to free childcare 28, 31–2, 33–4, 42
entry powers and consent 103–4
equalities targets 17
ethnic minorities 7, 30
Every Child Matters (ECM) 10, 15–16
exemptions
     compulsory OCR 92–3
     Early Years Foundation Stage 81–2
     Early Years Register 92
     registration 65–7
extended school services 8
EYFS *see* Early Years Foundation Stage
EYR *see* Early Years Register

failure to register 66, 67
false statements 107
fees for registration 109–10
financial provisions 123
flexibility 2
Foundation Stage Profile (FSP) 16, 18, 117
free childcare 28, 31–2, 33–4, 42, 116
FSP *see* Foundation Stage profile

goals of early learning 76
guidance 16, 36–8

HMRC, information for 105–6

improvement
     strategies 17–18
     targets 17
     well-being 1, 12, 14–18, 49
independent schools 82
individuals 59
inequalities reduction 1, 14
information
     to authorities 105–6
     collection 116–17
     disclosure 106–7
     to parents 13, 38–40, 51
     to/from providers 40, 117–18
     from registration applicants 69–70
inspections 5–6
     early years 83–4
     history 54
     later years 91
     Ofsted 41, 84–5
     reports 85–6, 91
     Wales 52
inspectors 9
     see also Chief Inspector
Isles of Scilly 123

later years provision 61

definition 113
inspections 91
regulation 87–91
upper age limit 61, 93
later years register 5
learning and development 75–8, 80, 81
legislation 120–2
listening to young children 22, 23–4
local authorities
     charges for childcare 34–5
     cooperation with partners/providers 24–5, 33–4, 51, 111
     definition 122–3
     duties 8, 45–6
          assessment 35–8
          childcare provision 26–31
          early childhood services 19–24
          information, advice and assistance 13, 38–40, 51, 105–6
          Wales 50
          well-being of children 14–18
     powers 32–3, 50
     target setting 16–17

misleading statements 107
mothers, working 2
multiple premises 112

nannies 9, 65
non-maintained providers 4
notices 111–12
OCR *see* Ofsted Childcare Register
Ofsted 9, 54, 60–3, 84–5, 105
Ofsted Childcare Register (OCR) 5–6, 7, 56, 63, 107–9, 110
     see also compulsory OCR registration; voluntary OCR registration
older children (5–14 years) 5, 8, 56, 93, 94
     see also later years provision

parenting classes 39
parents 2
     helping into work 28
     identification and encouragement 22, 23
     information, advice and assistance 8, 38–40, 51
     involvement 22, 23
     see also working parents
payment *see* charges
person, definition 58–9
police powers of entry 104
poverty reduction 3
powers
     of amendment 25
     of entry 103, 104
     local authorities 32–3, 50

powers *contd*
    Secretary of State 41, 96
    Welsh Assembly 52
pre-school groups *see* early years provision
private sector 33–4
process of registration 67–8
proper performance 41, 52
protection in an emergency 99–100
providers
    childcare 51, 93
    early years 9, 70–1, 73, 89
    information, advice and assistance 40, 117–18
    involvement 22
    local authority arrangements 33–4
    registration requirements 64–70

quality assurance schemes 34
quality of childcare 1, 3, 30–1
quantity of childcare places 3

registers 55–6, 62–3, 69–72, 99
registration
    appeals 101
    applications 68, 70–1, 88–9, 94
    cancellation 97
    certificates 71–2, 89, 95, 111
    childminders 66, 70–1, 87–8, 93, 94
    conditions 73, 90, 95
    disqualification 101–3, 119–20
    exemptions 65–7
    failure 66, 67
    fees 109–10
    history 54
    multiple premises 112
    notices 111–12
    procedures and notice period 95, 100–1
    process 67–8
    provision 57–8
    requirements 64–70
    safeguards 100
    suspension 98–9
    see also compulsory OCR registration; voluntary OCR registration
regulation(s) 5–6, 53–114
    activities 90–1, 95–6
    assessment 36–8
    early years provision 61, 64–86
    later years provision 87–91
Regulatory Impact Assessment (RIA) 6–7

removal from register 99
reporting, Ofsted 62
reports 85–6, 91, 104, 105
RIA *see* Regulatory Impact Assessment

schools
    charges 42
    extended services 8
    independent 82
    registration exemption 66–7
    status 112
Schools Census 116
Secretary of State's powers 41, 96
start dates 5, 7, 14, 35
sufficiency of provision 13, 28–9, 50
Sure Start Children's Centres 12, 21
Sure Start Local Programmes 3
suspension of registration 98–9
sustainability of provision 3–4, 31

target setting 16–17
'taught' debate 76–7
Ten Year Childcare Strategy 1, 2–3, 4, 55
time limits 108

unincorporated association offences 108–9
voluntary OCR registration 92–6
    childminders 93, 94
    children over 8 years 9
    nature and termination 93–5, 99
    start date 5, 7
voluntary sector 33–4

Wales 48–52, 118–19
Welfare Regulations 79–80
welfare requirements 79–80
well-being improvement 1, 12, 14–18, 49
Welsh Assembly 49, 52
Welsh language 50, 51
workforce 4–5, 8
working parents 2, 3, 13, 26–31, 50
Working Tax Credit 29, 50

young children (0–5 years) 7–8
    definition 44
    information about 117–19
    listening to 22, 23–4
    see also early years provision